Grace: The Truth, Growth, and Different Degrees

In 15 Sermons

by

Christopher Love
Minister of St. Lawrence Jewry, London

Edited by Rev. Don Kistler

Soli Deo Gloria Publications
. . . for instruction in righteousness . . .

Soli Deo Gloria Publications
P.O. Box 451, Morgan, PA 15064
(412) 221-1901/FAX 221-1902

*

*

ISBN 1-57358-034-1

Contents

Sermon 1

"Because in him there is found some good thing toward the Lord God of Israel, in the house of Jeroboam." 1 Kings 14:13

This chapter contains Ahijah's prophecy, foretelling what dismal judgments would befall Jeroboam and his posterity for his idolatry in worship and defection from the government and house of David. For these sins God destroyed him, and his posterity for their father's guilt; for so it is intimated in this verse, out of which the text is taken. Here was a young man, Jeroboam's son, who would die for the father's fault; and yet here was a mitigation of the punishment, that he should not die after the same manner that the rest did: "He shall go to his grave in peace, because in him there is found some good." Behold the goodness of God! A little good in him, and yet the great God takes notice of the little good. God found (as it were) one pearl in a heap of peoples, one good young man in Jeroboam's household, some good in him towards the Lord God of Israel.

In the whole verse, there are three parts:

1. A lamentation for the death of this son of Jeroboam. It is said, "All of Israel shall mourn for him," and so they did (verse 18), which argued there was goodness in him; for if he had not been desired and prized while he lived he would not have been so lamented at his death.

2. A limitation of his punishment. He only of Jeroboam's family shall come to the grave; the rest of his posterity who died in the city dogs would eat, and he who died in the field should the fowls of the air devour (verse 11).

3. The commendation of his life: "In him was found some good." Of this I am now to treat.

He is commended by the Holy Ghost, for his goodness is set forth:

By the quality of his goodness. It was a good thing, not a word only, or a good purpose of inclination with which too many content themselves, but it was a good action.

By the quantity of his goodness. It was but some little good thing that was found in him, and yet that little good God did not despise or overlook.

By the sincerity of his goodness. There are two notable demonstrations of this young man's goodness: it was towards the Lord God of Israel, and it was in Jeroboam's house.

His goodness was towards the Lord God of Israel. The Apostle Paul's sincerity was evidenced in that in his speaking, writing, and actions he could and did appeal to God. That religion, said the Apostle James, "is pure and undefiled" that is so "before God and the Father" (James 1:27). Many hypocrites may be good towards men who are not so towards God; to be rich indeed is to be rich towards God. True repentance is repentance towards God, and he is unblamable indeed who is void of offense towards God as well as towards men.

He was good in the house of Jeroboam. A wicked man may seem good in a good place, but to be good in a bad place argues men to be good indeed. To be good in David's house was not so much, but for this young man to be good in the house of Jeroboam his father —whom the Scripture brands for his idolatry in that "he made all Israel to sin," and yet who could not make his son to sin—argued he was sincerely good. As it argued Lot's sincerity to be righteous in Sodom, for Job to be good in Chaldea, and to be saints in Nero's palace, so to fear God in Jeroboam's family is goodness indeed.

There is only one difficulty in the text. What was that good thing that was found in Abijah?

For an answer to this, it is true the Scripture does not particularly express what that good thing was which was found in him, but Testatus and Peter Martyr affirm from the Hebrew rabbis that when the Jews of the ten tribes on their appointed times repaired to Jerusalem to worship according to the command of God, and Jeroboam commanded soldiers to intercept them, this Abijah hindered the soldiers from killing them, gave them passes to go to Jerusalem to worship God, and encouraged them therein, notwithstanding the rage of his father who had forsaken the true worship of God and set up calves at Dan and Bethel.

Others think the goodness of this young prince was that he would not consent to his father in taking away the government from the house of David. But where the Scripture has no tongue to speak, we must have no ear to hear; and therefore we shall not undertake to determine what the Scripture has not determined.

There are many collateral observations which I shall deduce from the several circumstances in the text, and but name some of them. From the consideration of what this good Abijah did, observe:

Good and useful men, and hopeful instruments, may be taken away by death, while wicked men may live long upon the earth.

Bad Jeroboam lived long; his good son died soon. So true is that verse of Solomon: "A righteous man may perish in his righteousness, when a wicked man may prolong his days in his wickedness" (Ecclesiastes 7:15); briars and thorns and thistles wither not so soon as lilies and roses. They may be taken out of the world of whom the world is not worthy, and they remain behind who are not worthy to live in the world.

From the consideration of the death of godly Abijah, when wicked Nadab the other son of Jeroboam lived, observe that good children may be taken away by death from their parents, when ungodly children may live to be a shame and a curse to their parents.

The cause why this gracious young man died so soon was for his father's sins, as we may gather from verses 9–12. Good children as well as bad may be outwardly punished for the sins of their parents.

From all Israel's lamenting the death of this hopeful young man, observe that good men who have been and might be further useful in their lives should be much lamented at their death; they who have lived desired should die lamented.

From these words, "he shall go to his grave in peace," observe that it is a great blessing to go to one's grave in peace, in times of war and common calamity.

"He was good towards God." He is good, indeed, who is so to God as well as to men; many are good in man's sight who are not so in the sight of God.

There are two other circumstances upon which I

shall a little enlarge myself before I come to the main point I intend to handle.

As for the age of this son of Jeroboam, who is here commended for his goodness, it is said he was a child (verse 12), from whence it may be observed that it is very commendable to see goodness in young people; to see young men be good men is a very commendable thing.

There were many good men in that time, but to be good so soon as Abijah was, when he was a child, the Scripture records this to his praise.

I shall show you that it is a commendable thing to see young men be good men. This I prove, first, because the Scripture makes very honorable mention of young men when they are good men. Obadiah feared the Lord from his youth. It is recorded to the honor of Timothy that he knew the holy Scriptures as a child. Jerome conceives that John was the most beloved disciple because he was the youngest of all. God remembers the kindness of our youth. God takes more kindly the kindness of our youth than of our age. It was a matter of joy unto John that he found children walking in the truth.

Second, God commends moral and common goodness in the young man in the gospel (Luke 10). Christ is said to love him for his moral goodness and natural ingenuity.

The reason why it is so commendable in a young man to be a good man is that their temptations are greater and their affections are stronger to carry them from God. Youth has a stronger aptitude and proclivity to sin than any other age; their blood is sooner stirred up to anger and their strength to lust. As every relation has its special sin, so it is in every age of a man's life. Old age is peevish and covetous; middle age proud, malicious, and vengeful; young men are usually rash, lustful, and voluptuous; and therefore Paul bids Timothy "flee all youthful lusts." Therefore, seeing that youth is exposed to so many temptations, and subject to so many corruptions, it is rare to see young men good.

Oh, then, be exhorted, you who are young, to become religious quickly, and to quicken you hereunto:

Consider, if you are not good in your youth, you can never use the Psalmist's argument: "for Thou art my hope, and hast been my trust from my youth" (Psalm 71:5). Who would be without such an argument on his death bed!

Consider, there are recorded in Scripture many young men who were good, of all sorts and conditions and of all callings; and the Holy Ghost not only sets down their goodness, but the age in which they were good: Solomon a young king, Obadiah a young courtier, Daniel a young prophet, and here Abijah a young prince. All these were good young men, and are recorded for our example and encouragement.

Consider that God, in the dispensations of His grace, bestows it upon young men, and passes by the elder. Thus Abel, the younger, was righteous and Cain wicked; Jacob the younger brother loved and Esau hated. David was the youngest of Jesse's sons, and yet the best of them, and the chosen of the Lord.

God many times does as Jacob did. When he blessed the children of Joseph, "he stretched out his hand, and laid it upon the head of Ephraim the younger" (Genesis 48:14). So God, in the dispensation of His grace, many times pitches upon the youngest. God says, as Joseph, of all the rest, "bring me Benjamin," and gives him a double portion.

The time of your youth is the freest age of your life to give yourselves to the exercise of religion and duties of godliness. Young men who are servants have more freedom and fewer cares than when they grow in years, when the cares and encumbrances of a family fill their hands and clog their hearts.

Consider, if you are not gracious in your youth, the sins of your youth may trouble your conscience in your old age. Many young men who are active and adventurous in the heat of their youth get those bodily bruises and blows that they feel the ache thereof to their dying day. You who give a blow or bruise to your conscience in your youth may feel this in your old age.

Those sins which now you feel not may be a trouble to your conscience, and an aching to your heart, when you lie on your deathbed. And though God does not remember the sins of your youth to damn your souls, yet He may make you remember them so as to be a trouble to your consciences.

These things which are the joys of youth may be the bitter burdens of old age. Take heed of laying a load on your conscience when you are young lest God write bitter things against you when old, and make you to possess the sins of your youth, and fill your bones with the sins of your youth.

USE OF REPROOF. This is for two sorts of people:

First, of those who, instead of being good when young, are wicked when they are young, such as fill their youth with manifold evils. Usually youth is subject to these evils.

Pride is the sin of youth; a preacher must not be a young novice, lest he be lifted up with pride.

Rashness and indiscretion are usually the sins of a young head. "Exhort young men (said Paul to Titus) to be sober-minded, to be discreet and wise" (Titus 2:6). How rash and heady was the counsel of the young men to Rehoboam, which made him lose his kingdom! Years teach experience.

Lustfulness was the ground of Paul's caution to young Timothy. If Timothy, who was so abstemious a man that Paul gave him advice to drink some wine with his water, had need of this caution, how much more have they who are not so exercised in duties of mortification? This gave Solomon ground to give that counsel: "put away the evils of the flesh, for childhood and youth are vanity" (Ecclesiastes 11:10). He was a young man who followed the harlot to her house.

Youth also tend toward sickliness and unsettledness of judgment; and therefore, in times of error, the younger sort are most subject to be seduced. Children are tossed to and fro with "every wind of doctrine" (Ephesians 4:14). The Hebrew signifies "to toss to and fro," intimating that they are unsettled and unstayed in their judgments and resolutions. How soon was the mind of that rich and forward young man mentioned in the gospel changed?

Youth often scoff and condemn the aged; they were children who mocked the aged prophet; the young men derided Job.

Youth are vulnerable to sensual pleasures and pastimes; they rejoice and cheer their hearts in the days of their youth. "Samson made a feast, for so used the young men to do" (Judges 14:10).

Reproof lights heavily on those who seem to be good in their youth, but in their old age cast off goodness. How many are like Joash, who seemed to be a good young man while he was under the tuition of Jehoiada; but when he was dead, how did he break out?

How many are there in the world who have lost the affections and desires after God they had in their youth? It was a brand set upon Solomon that, though when young he was well taught by his mother, yet when he grew old his wives turned away his heart from God. So David had his first days, which were better than his last.

Even so among us, we have too many who, when they were young, loved religion and delighted in ordinances, and when they became old have abated exceedingly, which may make them fear the sincerity of their goodness. For he who is truly good in youth will be so in his old age.

A second remarkable circumstance is that this young Abijah was good in the house of Jeroboam. Whence observe that it is a great commendation for men to retain their goodness while they live in bad places and families. That it is so we may see by that commendable mention the Scriptures make of such as were good in evil places. Thus God commends the church of Pergamus: "I know thy works, and where thou dwellest, even where Satan's seat is; and thou holdest fast My name, and hast not denied My faith, even in those days wherein Antipus was My faithful martyr, who was slain amongst you, where Satan dwelleth." Pergamus was a city more given to idolatry than all the cities of Asia, and yet there were some who held fast the name of Christ and did not deny His faith. To be a saint in Nero's family is very commendable.

And the reason thereof is:

1. Because many of God's children have failed and abated much of their goodness in bad places. How did Peter fall in the high priest's hall? When in good company he was zealous, yet there he denied Christ. So Abraham, when he was in Gerar, and Isaac also, denied their wives. Joseph in Pharaoh's court had learned the court oath, to swear by the life of Pharaoh. Hence God commanded the children of Israel not to mix themselves with the heathens lest they learn their manners and customs. Bad places are like bad air for zeal to breathe in. As sheep among briars lose part of their fleece, so good men in bad company lose part of their goodness. As one scabbed sheep may infect a whole flock, so no root of bitterness may spring up without defiling many.

2. Because it is a clear evidence of the sincerity of a man's goodness to be good in a bad place. This shows your grace to be grace indeed, when you have discouragements to be good and still are holy. This is a demonstration that you are sincerely good, and that your goodness is not counterfeit and taken up on any sinister and hypocritical end. It is good to be good with the good, but it is most excellent to be good among the bad, and to be best among the worst.

From hence learn the power and unlooseableness of favoring grace. Grace keeps a man good in the worst times. Let a man be cast into prison or bad company (which is the worst temptation), yet he shall not lose his grace. Grace is compared to oil; now carry oil into a vessel of water and the oil will not mix with the water but will lie on the top. Grace will swim upon the water of temptation. As all the water in the salt sea cannot make the fish salty, so all the wickedness in the world cannot change the nature of grace. A good man like the fish retains his goodness in bad places. Thus Joseph retained his goodness in the court of wicked Pharaoh, Nehemiah in the court of Artaxerxes, Obadiah in Ahab's court, Daniel in Nebuchadnezzar's, the saints in Nero's household, and Abijah in wicked and idolatrous Jeroboam's house.

Though it is a commendable thing to be good in bad places, yet you ought to bewail your living in bad places; it is your misery though not your sin. Thus did Isaiah: "Woe is me, I am undone; because I am a man of unclean lips, and I dwell in the midst of unclean lips" (Isaiah 6:5). So did David: "Woe is me that I dwell in Meshech, and have my habitation in the tents of Kedar" (Psalm 120:5), i.e., with sinful, idolatrous, and barbarous people, the posterity of Ishmael. Thus Lot's righteous soul was vexed from day to day while he dwelt in Sodom, "and saw their unclean conversations."

Hence we may gather that it is our duty. The worse the place or family is where God has cast your dwelling, the better and more blameless you should labor to be. You will by this adorn your profession, stop the mouths of adversaries, and allure and win others to embrace Christianity. We must be "blameless and harmless, the sons of God, without rebuke, in the midst of a crooked and perverse nation, amongst whom ye shine as lights in the world" (Philippians 2:15). Stars shine brightest in a dark night, and fire burns hottest in a cold and frosty day. So should your star of profession shine brightest in dark places where you live, and the fire of your zeal burn hottest in cold times, when the love of many waxes cold.

Then certainly it is a vain plea for men to excuse their wickedness because they live in bad places. This was Abraham's fault, to excuse his lie by being at Gerar. Seneca blames men for laying the fault of their badness on the place where they live. "I am not ambitious by nature, but no man who lives at Rome can be otherwise. I am not given to costly and rich apparel, but I must do so when I am in Rome." It is the badness of your heart, and not the place, that makes you bad. No place, though never so good, can exempt a man from sin. The angels sinned in heaven, Adam in paradise, Judas in Christ's family. And no place, though never so bad, can excuse a man from sin.

If it is so commendable to be good in bad places, then it is abominable to be bad in good places, to be a dirty swine in a fair meadow. Oh, how many are bad in good families, who despise good counsels and hate the duties of religion in religious families! If it was bad for Peter to be evil among the high priest's servants, how abominable was it for Judas to be a traitor among the apostles, and in the family of Christ Himself!

Delight not to be in bad places and company; to delight in such argues you are bad yourself. We are to hate the garment spotted with the flesh. Some expound this, "to avoid the occasions of sin," but Mr. [William] Perkins gives this sense: "to hate bad company." He says it alludes to the ceremonial law that said that if a man had a leprous garment, or a garment otherwise made unclean, his company was to be avoided. God therefore gave that command not to plow with an ox and an ass together; the ass was an unclean creature, and the ox was one of the clean beasts, and they must not be in the same yoke. This notes (say divines) that God's people and profane persons must not be yoked together. Though they may occasionally meet together, yet they must not be yoked together. A man may trade with the wickedest man alive—commerce is not forbidden—but our joining with wicked men in a needless familiarity is forbidden.

Keep company with the godly and delight your-selves with such as are good. It is lawful to be in bad company when a just occasion calls, but it is profitable to be in good company. "He that walketh with wise men shall be wise, but he that is a companion of fools shall be destroyed" (Proverbs 13:20). As a man who comes unto a shop of perfumes will carry away the scent with him, so a man, by conversing with the godly, shall carry away some good with him. Labor to choose those for your companions from whom you may get some good; but if God should cast you into a house like the family of Jeroboam, imitate good Abijah, of whom it is said that in him was found some good to the Lord God of Israel, even in the house of Jeroboam.

Sermon 2

"Because in him there is found some good thing toward the Lord God of Israel, in the house of Jeroboam." 1 Kings 14:13

Having dispatched the observations which may be gathered from the circumstances of the text, **I come to the main doctrine I intend to handle: God not only exactly takes notice of, but also tenderly cherishes and graciously rewards, the smallest beginnings and weakest measures of grace which He works in the hearts of His own people.**

I might produce a cloud of testimonies to confirm this point. Our Savior Christ said that He will not "break the bruised reed, nor quench the smoking flax" (Matthew 12:20). Observe, the bruised reed shall not be broken; not the light and flaming torch, but the smoking flax shall not be quenched. Smoking flax, where there is but little fire, and much smoke of infirmity, yet Christ will not quench it. He will cherish it. Here less is spoken than is intended. He will be so far from quenching that He will cherish the smoking flax, as in another place God says that He "will not despise a broken heart" (Psalm 51:17). Rather, He will highly esteem it.

Solomon speaks of the fig tree putting forth her green figs, and the vine with her tender grapes giving a good smell. That is, the little measure and weak beginnings of grace in young converts please the Lord Jesus

Christ, and are as a sweet smell in His nostrils. Again, Christ said, "Let us see if the vine flourish, whether the tender grapes appear, and the pomegranate bud forth" (Song of Solomon 7:12). The green buds are regarded by Christ as well as the ripe and grown fruit.

In opening the doctrine, I shall endeavor to show these two things: Some of God's people have but weak measures and small beginnings of grace. But second, though there is but a little grace, yet God will regard and reward it.

First, some of God's people have but a little grace; they have but the beginnings of grace wrought in their souls. In the handling of this there are three things:

The truth of the proposition may be made good from the Scriptures.

I will lay down notes of discovery to such as have but small measures of grace wrought in them.

And then I will show why God in His wisdom will not suffer His people to be all of an equal strength and stature in grace.

QUESTION. How does it appear that some of God's people are but weak in grace?

ANSWER 1. By the different names and titles that are given unto Christians in the holy Scriptures, arguing they are of different measure and growth in grace. Some are called strong men and others weak. Some are called babes in Christ and others grown men. Some are called trees of righteousness, plants of renown, that grow like cedars in Lebanon, and others are but a bruised reed. Some are kids in Christ's flock, and lambs. Others are as the he-goats, that go stately before the flock. Some have grace flaming forth in much zeal and vivacity; they have the spirit of burning; and others are but "smoking flax," Christians who have much of the smoke of infirmity and but little of the flame of grace.

ANSWER 2. By the analogy that is between spiritual and natural differences of age, strength, and stature in man. The holy Scripture exactly sets down all the different degrees of grace under the similitude of the different ages of men. There is a forming of Christ in the heart, and so a spiritual conception. There are some who are but newborn babes in Christ.

There are some who are advanced from infancy to be young men. There are some who are grown men in Christ, old men. And all this but sets forth the different degrees of grace that are in Christians, some having less and some more.

In the church of Christ, which is His orchard, there are trees of all sorts, spikenard and saffron, calamus and cinnamon, with all trees of frankincense, myrrh and aloes (see Song of Solomon 4:14). [Daniel] Brightman, commenting on this Scripture, notes that hereby is meant the several sorts of Christians. Spikenard and saffron are young, weak professors; these are tender plants that scarcely lift up the head above the ground. Calamus and cinnamon, which are shrubs of two cubits high, denote Christians of a middle size; and the other trees denote Christians of a more eminent measure, and growth in grace.

QUESTION. How may a man know himself that he is but of a little measure, and small beginning in grace?

ANSWER 1. To be much in dependence on duties argues you are but weak in grace. A young Christian is like a young carpenter: he makes many chips, and has many blows, but does not make such smooth work as an experienced carpenter, who will make fewer chips, and at fewer blows better work. So young children are much in the use of duty, but they are apt to rely upon duty. They think duties make them saints, and they are apt to make saviors of their duties and be frequent in their duties. They see not their failings in their duties, and so are apt to rest on their duties. As it is a sign of an apostate professor to call off duty, so it is also a note of a young and weak professor to rest too much upon his duties.

ANSWER 2. A weak Christian does not have clear insight into the close and spiritual failings which cleave to his performances. He sees his gifts, and takes notice of his affections, but he does not see the vanity of his mind, the unsoundness of his ends, his carnal dependence upon his duty, self-love, and vainglory; but in the course of time, a grown Christian takes notice of these things in himself. An experienced Christian will take as much notice of his failing in duty as of his ability in it; and though he discerns an enlargement of gifts and graces in himself at times, yet he still discerns much spiritual pride, popular applause, ostentation of gifts, and too much forwardness in setting out his parts, which a weak Christian seldom perceives.

ANSWER 3. To have a scrupulous conscience about matters of indifference argues a weak Christian; for so the Apostle calls them "weak in the faith," such as bound conscience when the Scripture left it free. One believer thought he might eat anything, and another doubted the lawfulness of eating sundry things. Now those who doubted, the Apostle called weak; and the weak conscience is apt to be defiled. Not to know our liberty, and to abuse our liberty, is an argument we have but little grace. Young converts call more things sins than ever God did; they perplex and entangle themselves merely in indifferent things. It is true, there ought to be a conscientious tenderness in all Christians; tenderness of conscience is our duty, but a tormenting, entangling scrupulosity is our infirmity. And yet, as a weak Christian is better than no Christian, a weak faith is better than a seared conscience.

ANSWER 4. To be so intently set on the exercises of religion, as to neglect our particular callings is a sign we are but weak in grace. It was a good saying of that famous man of God, Dr. [Richard] Sibbes: "I like that Christian well that will hear much and live much, that will pray much and work much." In young converts, the affections are strong and stirring, and they think they can never hear enough. Many times they neglect the duties of their callings, which argues their weakness and infirmity. An experienced, grown Christian is regular in his general and particular callings, so that the one shall not jostle and hinder the others.

ANSWER 5. To have men's persons in admiration argues weakness in grace. Such were the Corinthians. The Apostle called them children, babes; though they had the life of Christians, yet they had but little of the strength of Christians. They were carnal; they favored the flesh more than the Spirit. Ignorance is often a cause of admiration. Weak Christians who have but little knowledge are apt to be so taken with men's persons that one cries, "I am of Paul," and another, "I am of Apollos," and so they fall into sin, condemned of combining the faith of Christ with respect of persons, so as to cry up one minister and cry down others. To idolize some, and to despise others, argues that you are in weak faith. A solid Christian loves all good ministers and can condemn none.

ANSWER 6. To be easily seduced and led away into error argues weakness in grace. The Apostle Paul calls those children who are "tossed to and fro and carried about with every wind of doctrine" (Ephesians 4:14). Weakness of head argues that grace is not very strong in your heart. The way not to fall from our steadfastness is to grow in grace, for the Apostle Peter joins these two duties together. Having given caution in 2 Peter 3:17 "not to fall from steadfastness," in verse 18 he gives counsel "to grow in grace." Strong Christians are steadfast, whereas weak ones are inconstant; and therefore, as for those professors who have been whirled about with divers opinions, it is an evidence they have but weak grace, if any.

ANSWER 7. Such as are only acquainted with the common principles of religion, without further search into the depths and mysteries of religion, are weak in grace. There are some professors who may be fitly called babes in Christ because they need milk, being unskillful in the word of righteousness, that is, in the more solid doctrines of the gospel concerning Christ who is our righteousness. Thus the disciples and apostles of Christ knew but little of our redemption at first, and were ignorant concerning the passion of Christ— of the resurrection, as also of the affection of Christ— till the Holy Ghost came and taught them these things, and brought those things to remembrance that Christ had taught them.

ANSWER 8. Weak Christians are strong in affections and not in judgment; they have usually more heat than light. Young Christians are like young horses: they have much mettle, but are not so fit for a journey because they are not so thoroughly trained. There are many Christians who have much zeal and affection, but are not solid in their judgment. This argues much weakness in grace.

ANSWER 9. A weak Christian is one who cannot bear reproof. Sharp weather discovers whether you are of a weak or sound body. So a sharp reproof will discover whether you are of a weak spiritual temper and constitution. When Nathan came to David, he could bear the reproof though the prophet told him to his face that he was the man who had sinned. Asa, though a good man, could not endure the faithful reproof of a prophet, but was wroth with the seer and put him in the prison house.

ANSWER 10. A weak believer is one who can trust God for his soul, but not for his body. So Jesus Christ argued of those who had little faith, who expected heaven and happiness from God their Father, and trusted Him with their souls and eternal concerns, and yet dared not trust Him for food and raiment. There are those who dare trust God for heaven, and yet do not trust Him for earth, but these are of little faith. When the disciples wanted bread, they began to reason among themselves how they should be supplied. "O ye of little faith," said Christ, "why do you thus reason? Can you trust Me for the bread of eternal life, and dare you not trust Me for the bread of this life?"

Be not then discouraged, you who discern in yourselves but small measures of grace; look on your wants and imperfections so as to grow in grace, and not to be content with any measure, but look not on the small beginnings in grace as discouragement to you. When you see a great oak in a field, you may say this great tree was once but a small acorn. Those Christians who now are but small sprigs may hereafter be tall cedars. Say to your soul, "Though I am but weak, yet I shall be strong." Grace, where it is true, will be growing; the smoking flax may be a burning and shining lamp in God's candlestick. And therefore, as you may not be content with the greatest measure of grace, so neither be discouraged with the least measure of grace. A grain of mustard seed may grow a great tree.

Content not yourselves with small measures of grace. A little of the world will not content you. In the womb a foot contents us, three feet in the cradle, and seven feet in the grave. But between the cradle and the grave, a whole world will not content us; and shall a little grace content us? For wealth and desire of it, you are as the horse leech that cries, "Give, give," and as the grave that never says, "It is enough," and for grace, will you be content with a little?

Sermon 3

"Because in him there is found some good thing toward the Lord God of Israel, in the house of Jeroboam." 1 Kings 14:13

We have given some Scriptural examples of those who have a little grace; now we proceed to resolve a third question.

QUESTION. Why does God so order and ordain it that, among His own people, all shall not be of an equal stature in Christ, but there are some of them in whom there are but the beginnings of grace found?

ANSWER. It is true, it is not with regeneration as it was in the creation; it is not with the trees of righteousness as it was with the trees of paradise which were created all perfect at first. But it is not so in the work of grace. We are not perfectly sanctified, nor all at once, but we are perfecting holiness in the fear of God, and that by degrees. God has given to some of His people but small beginnings and measures of grace, and that for these reasons.

1. To put a difference between our state on earth and our being in heaven. In heaven we shall all have an equal stature in grace, though it is disputed whether there are different degrees of glory. But in heaven the "spirits of just men" shall all be "made perfect" (Hebrews 12:23), and there we shall all come unto the "measure of the stature of the fullness of Christ" (Ephesians 4:13). All believers are here justified by

God alike. God does not acquit the strong and hold guilty the weak, but justification is alike to all. Our sanctification shall be then as our justification is now, that is, perfect and equal; we shall have not only a perfection of parts, but of degrees.

2. This is to make men live in a continual dependence upon divine influx, and supplies from the Spirit of God. If children should be born perfect men, as Adam was created, we would not then see that continual need of, and dependence on, our parents. We are bred in the womb, and afterwards born into the world, and then by degrees grow up from stature to stature; and so it is in grace. God deals thus. Converting grace does not make us as perfect as we shall be afterward. At the first creation He made the trees all fruitful and fully grown; but now it is otherwise, for they are first kernels or seeds, then plants before they are grown trees; and they have dependence on the influences of heaven. So we are first babes, then young men, and then strong men in Christ, to keep our souls in a dependence on God's grace.

3. For the greater ornament of the mystical body of Christ. In a natural body, if every member should be of an equal size, the body would be monstrous; but the body is so proportioned in its different members that the lesser ones become serviceable to the greater, and so they all discharge their mutual operations in orderly fashion. In music there would be no harmony if the strings were all of an equal size; but one string being the bass and the other the treble makes the music to be more melodious. So it is in grace: the different degrees of grace make the body of Christ more harmonious. It is here as in some curious piece of needle-

work: if all the silks were of one color, it would not set
out the work with so much luster and amiableness as
the variety of colors will do.

4. To make God's people see a necessity of maintaining fellowship and communion together, to edify
and build up each other. There would be no need of
Christian discourse and holy fellowship did not our
weakness require it. As among the members of the
body, God has so ordered them that each member is
serviceable to another—"the eye cannot say to the
hand, I have no need of thee" (1 Corinthians 12:21)—
so among the people of God, some being weak and
others strong, there is a necessity of maintaining communion together. There is an instinct in nature that
things weak in themselves cleave to those things which
are stronger than they. The conies are but a feeble
folk, yet make their houses in the rocks; among birds,
the dove is the silliest and most shiftless creature, yet
hides herself in the clefts of the rock. The vine among
the trees is the weakest, yet it clings to the wall; the
hops among the plants, yet they twine about the pole.
So God has ordered it in His infinite wisdom that some
Christians should be stronger and some weaker in
grace, that the strong may help the weak, and each be
serviceable to one another.

5. To set out the glory of God in all His glorious attributes.

This different size of grace in Christians glorifies
the mercy and the free grace of God, who, when there
are some Christians who have but a little grace, yet rewards those small measures of grace with great measures of glory.

This magnifies the power of God who, when we are

weak, yet manifests His power in our weakness, yea, His "strength is made perfect in weakness" (2 Corinthians 12:9). And therefore Paul adds in verse 10: "For when I am weak, then am I strong," that is, strong in Christ. Is it not a demonstration of great powers to keep a small spark of fire so that it shall not be quenched in a flood of water? Yet behold, that little spark of grace in you shall not be quenched by the flood and torrent of your corruption. It is by God's power that the least measure of grace shall be preserved. There is not so much of God's power seen in preserving the angels as in a weak believer, for the angels, though mutable, yet are perfect creatures; they have no weights of sin and corruption to pull them down. But alas! We have such a bias and inclination to sin that we are apt to be turned aside from God every moment. The power of God is more seen in preserving a poor believer in the state of grace than in preserving the angels in the state of innocence.

And as God's power is seen in preserving a little grace, so it is also seen in the increasing of small grace. Grace is like that cloud, which the prophet's servant saw, which at first "was but like a man's hand," but afterwards "it overspread the whole heaven." True grace is of a spreading and increasing nature; and therefore the increase of our graces may be sketched out in the vision of the waters of the sanctuary which at first were up to the ankles, after that to the knees, then to the loins, and at last so deep that they could not be passed over.

God hereby glorifies His wisdom. As God's wisdom is demonstrated in the world by the variety of creatures, which are not all of the same build and size, but some bigger and some lesser, so, in the church of God, His wisdom appears in that some Christians are of greater and some of a lesser measure of grace. Search the whole creation and you shall find the wisdom of God in the variety of creatures. In the heavens there are greater and lesser lights, and so stars of different magnitude beautify and bespangle the heavens. In the sea there are greater and lesser fishes; in the air, the great eagle and little sparrow; on the earth, the elephant and little dog; among the creeping things, there's the great serpent and the little ant; amongst the vegetables, the tall cedar and hyssop on the wall; among the rational creatures, there is a giant and a dwarf, a grown man of a tall stature and a child of but a span long. So God's wisdom is greatly illustrated in that there is variety of natural proportions of grace in His church among His children.

Before I come to apply this point, which is of very great use to God's children for their comfort, I shall lay down some general positions about small measures of grace.

In the church there are found more weak Christians than strong, more young converts than old and grown Christians. In a forest, there are more young sprouts than old trees; in a garden more young flips than old roots; in the world, more young children than old men. In Nineveh there were 120,000 infants, but there was not such a number of old men. By how much things are perfect, by so much they are the fewer.

Look among other creatures: those that are of a bigger bulk are of a lesser number. In the sea, there are more young and little fish than great whales; on the earth, the smallest things are innumerable; in the air there are more swarms of flies than flocks of birds. So it is in the church of God: there are more young and weak converts than old Christians. It is with most Christians as it was with Jonathan's signal arrows which he shot to warn David by: two fell short and one went beyond the mark. So where one Christian shoots home to the mark of "the prize of the high calling of God in Christ Jesus" (Philippians 3:14), there are many who fall short.

There are many who have but weak measures and small beginnings of grace, who have been a long time under the profession of religion, and under the means of grace. Such were the Hebrews, who for the time that they ought to be teachers, yet had need that one should teach them again the first principles of the oracles of God, and were become such as had need of milk, and not of strong meat. And I may accommodate to this purpose that speech of Christ: "Many that are first shall be last, and the last shall be first."

There are many who went out early and took, as it were, the first step in the profession of religion; and yet others have overtaken them who went out after them. Many, who have but weak measures of grace, have been of long standing under the means of grace. And therefore Christians are not to judge the strength of grace by their profession, but by their proficiency; it is not how many years you have been professors, but what experience and judgment you have gotten under ordinances.

The smallest measures of grace cannot merit eternal life and glory, because *great* measures cannot. In merit there ought to be a proportion, but between grace and glory there is none. Our services are imperfect, our salvation is perfect; our services are but momentary, our glory is eternal. There is no comparison between our light duties and our eternal weight of glory. The church in the Song of Solomon is described according to the several parts of her body. Her voice is sweet, her countenance comely, and her dove's eyes are beautiful. "Behold, thou art fair, my love (said Christ), thou hast dove's eyes, thy cheeks are comely with rows of jewels, and thy neck with chains of gold" (Song of Solomon 1:10, 15). Now it is very observable that though Christ commends the church's eyes, her hair, her teeth, lips, and speech, her temples, her breasts, her neck, yet He does not commend her hands, to show that though she is adorned with many graces, as with so many beautiful ornaments and comely lineaments, yet she merits nothing from the hand of Christ by all her doings. The church's beauty is perfect through the comeliness of Christ.

Believers ought not to rest satisfied with the small measure of grace they have received. Though a little grace may bring you to heaven, yet you are not to take up therewith; but if you have gotten a little grace, labor for more.

And to quicken you hereunto, consider that small measures of grace are not so sensible and evidential to yourselves; little things, because they are little, are not seen. There may be a little dust hovering up and down in the air, yet because it is small we see it not. This is the reason why Christians doubt: grace is little, and therefore it is not discerned. Compare Matthew 8:26 with Mark 4:40, and you shall find that in Matthew Christ said, in His reproof to His disciples, "O ye of little faith!" and in Mark, "How is it that ye have no faith?" You may, from the variety of these expressions, gather that a little faith unexercised, as to comfort, is as good as no faith. It was so little, and weak grace may not further you in a way of a strong consolation. Not but that a weak Christian is accepted, and the weaker Christian may lie in his Father's bosom, yet it is the strength of grace that gives us strong consolation.

Consider that small measures of grace, though they may bring you to heaven, yet are not so useful to others. Weak Christians cannot do much good in Christian converse because they lack judgment and experience in the ways of God; and therefore such are not to be received to doubtful disputations, but are to be borne with. Spiritual and strong Christians are most useful.

Young converts are not fit for some exercises about religion; they are not yet fit to strengthen others. "When thou art converted, strengthen thy brethren" (Luke 22:32). It is not to be understood of Peter's first conversion, but of his profession in religion, as if Christ had said, "When you are strengthened yourself, strengthen your brethren."

There are some duties which young converts are not fit for. "A piece of new cloth is not fit for an old garment, neither old bottles fit for new wine." Pareus, along with most expositors, refers this place to that case of conscience: "Why did Christ's disciples not fast often?" They were like old and weak bottles, and so were not fit for that strong duty, which was as new wine and would be apt to break them. Christ said to His disciples that He had many things to say unto them which, in regard of their weakness, they were not then able to bear.

Nor are small measures of grace so honorable to God. God is glorified when His people bear much fruit. Much means and pains and little fruit is a shame to the vinedresser, and therefore believers must not rest satisfied with small measures of grace.

It is our duty to improve those small measures of grace which God has given us. And consider that he who is faithful in a little, God will make him ruler over much. Use of grace will increase it; yet if grace is increased, ascribe all to God. It is God's pound, and not your pains, that has gained.

USE OF COMFORT. This is to weak Christians, to those young Abijahs in whom there is found but little good. Let such know to their comfort:

1. Though your grace is but little in quantity, yet it is much in value. A pearl, though but little in substance, yet is of great worth; so a little grace is of great value. The heart of a wicked man is worth nothing. You may have much knowledge and seeming grace, but no true worth. A shop full of barrels will not make a man rich unless those vessels are full of commodities. Gifts, as to heaven, are but the lumber of a Christian; it is grace that makes him rich towards God.

2. Though your grace is little for the present, yet it will grow in the future to a greater measure. The little grain of mustard seed (the least of seeds) will in time grow up to a tree. Grace is fitly compared to leaven which is of a spreading nature, to the cloud which the prophet's servant saw, and to the waters of the sanctuary, which all increased. An infant of days shall proceed by degrees till he becomes like "the ancient of days," as perfect as his heavenly Father is perfect.

Naturalists observe that the seeds of the cypress tree
are very small, and yet of them proceeds a very high
tree. Such is the birth and growth of grace.

3. The little measure of grace once begun in the
soul shall be perfected. God will not "break the bruised
reed, nor quench the smoking flax, until judgment be
perfected in victory" (Matthew 12:20). By judgment is
meant the work of sanctification, till that comes to
prevail over corruption. Paul was confident that He
who began a good work in them would finish it unto
the day of Jesus Christ. The Lord is faithful and will do
it. God has commanded us to go on to perfection, and
He does not command impossibilities. God blames
men for folly in not proceeding to finish when they
have begun to build. God will never begin to rear up a
structure of grace and not finish it. Besides, God has
promised to perfect that which concerns His servants.

4. The weakest Christian has grace alike for quality,
though not for quantity. Though your grace is not so
much as others', yet it is as true as others'; though you
may be but converted yesterday, yet your grace is as
true as if you were an old stander in religion. Faith is
alike precious in all believers for quality, though not
for quantity.

Faith in all believers is alike in respect of the author, God. Faith in all believers is alike in respect of
the object it holds upon, the same Christ. Faith in all
believers is alike in respect that the means working it
are the same, the Word and Spirit. A little grace is true
grace. Fire in the spark is as much fire as the flame; the
filings of gold are gold as well as the whole lode. A little grace is true grace.

Faith in all believers is alike in that its end is the

same: the salvation of the soul (1 Peter 1:9).

God will not put your weak grace to trial beyond your strength. God will debate with it in measure. He will stay His rough wind in the day of His east wind. You shall not have such boisterous storms of temptations, as a stronger Christian. God will not suffer us to be tempted above what we are able. God will take care that the spirit does not fail.

Take this for your comfort: the least measure of grace is enough to bring you to heaven. This is not spoken to make you idle, but only to comfort a perplexed conscience. Many, because their grace is weak, think they have no grace. "I have set before thee (said Christ to the church of Philadelphia) an open door, and no man can shut it; for thou hast a little strength, and hast kept My word, and hast not denied My name" (Revelation 3:8). It is true, our comfort lies much in the comparative degree, but our salvation is in the positive degree. Strong grace has strong comfort. Much faith will bring you with much comfort to heaven, but a little faith will bring you safely to heaven.

Sermon 4

"Because in him there is found some good thing toward the Lord God of Israel, in the house of Jeroboam." 1 Kings 14:13

Before we come to the use of caution, I shall here state a case of conscience: If among God's people there are some found who have but little grace, small measures in them, then what is the least measure of grace less than which a man cannot be said to be in a state of grace?

This is a practical and useful case.

First, this is of great use to Christians who are but of a lower form in religion, and have but little grace. Yet they may know what little they have, and though they have not attained strength of grace, yet they may know the truth of grace in themselves. Although they come short of strong believers, yet they shall hereby know they go beyond the hypocrite; for the least measure of grace is better than the greatest measure of gifts.

Second, the knowledge of this will quicken the soul unto due endeavors after a further increase. This will teach them to "abound more and more." Now, that I may discover what is the lowest degree of true grace, I shall show you it in some of these following particulars:

1. A light in the soul to see the evil and mischievous nature of sin, though not an ability to mortify sin. The entrance of God's Word gives light and understanding to the simple; that is, the first work of the Word upon

the soul, the very beginning of converting grace in the heart is light, whereby you see sin and its sinfulness. As it was in the first creation, the first thing that was created was light; so in the second creation, the first work is "to open the eyes of the blind, and to turn them from darkness to light, and from the power of Satan to God." Upon the work of conversion in the soul, the first degree of grace is to be enlightened with the light of the living. So that where this light is wanting, there cannot be a work of grace.

2. A settled and fixed purpose of heart to leave sin and cleave unto God. Grace does not so much consist in an actual mortifying of sin as in an unfeigned and settled purpose of heart to leave every sin.

The prodigal's resolution to go to his father's house argued some grace in him. "I will arise and go to my father's house," he said; that is, "I will leave my wicked company and courses." And it is said, "his father saw him afar off, and ran and met him." The Lord worked in him a purpose to leave sin. Gregory on this place said, "The remission of sin came to his heart before his confession broke out in his speech to his father."

So it was with David: "I acknowledged my sin unto Thee, and mine iniquity have I not hid. I said, 'I will confess my transgression unto the Lord,' and Thou forgavest the iniquity of my sin" (Psalm 32:5). Augustine observed on this place that David did not say he confessed, but he *purposed* to confess his sin; and yet his purpose was true grace, though one of the least measures of grace. That holy purpose of David argued grace in him when he said, "I have purposed, and will not transgress Thy law. I have sworn, and will perform

it, that I will keep Thy righteous judgments." It argues
grace when a soul cleaves unto the Lord with full purpose of heart.

3. Another low but sufficient measure of grace is a
sensible complaint of the want of grace. Thus he who
came to Christ said with tears, "Lord, I believe, help
Thou my unbelief." He had grace. He did not say,
"Lord, help my faith," but "Lord, help my unbelief."
His expression about his unbelief noted not only his
want, but his sensibleness of his want. This is that
poverty of spirit which has the first place in the
Beatitudes; this is the lowest rung of the ladder. The
Apostle tells that "the Spirit helps our infirmities"
(Romans 8:26), in sighs and groans that cannot be
uttered. Observe that it is not said that the Spirit helps
us with comforts and joys, but with sighs and groans.
Whence we may learn that the Spirit's help is as well in
sighs and groans and sensible complaints of our wants
as in holy ravishments. Strength of grace is seen in holy
joys and ravishments of spirit, but truth of grace may
be seen and discerned in sighs and groans and complaints of our wants. They are said to be sighs and
groans which cannot be uttered, not in regard of their
greatness, but (as Mr. Perkins observes) in regard of
their weakness: God's children at first lack ability to
express their own thoughts. To be sensible of the want
of grace is grace, for nature cannot make a man duly
sensible of the want of grace, nor sensibly to complain
of that want.

4. Earnest desire after more grace argues there is
grace in the soul, though it is but small. I do not place
the beginning of grace in the ability to exercise grace;
but it is rather an earnest desire after grace. Desire af-

ter grace is accounted by God as the grace itself we desire; for so we find that Nehemiah's desire to fear the
Lord is counted for actually fearing God. Desires are
the seeds of grace, and the graces themselves are the
blossoms and sweet fruits that spring from thence;
grace exercised is the fruit of a holy desire after grace.

That the desire after grace is, in God's acceptance,
itself grace may be thus demonstrated.

God's people have appealed unto God, concerning
the uprightness of their hearts, merely by their desires.
So said the church: "The desire of our soul is to Thy
name, and the remembrance of Thee, and with my
soul have I desired Thee in the night" (Isaiah 26:8–9).

God has many gracious promises not only to the
acting and exercising of grace, but to the desires after
grace. "Blessed are they that hunger and thirst after
righteousness; for they shall be filled." And "If any man
thirst let him come unto Me and drink." Nay, there is a
general and universal invitation to everyone who thirsts
to come to the waters; and God has promised to give
"to him that is athirst, of a fountain of the water of life
freely" (Revelation 21:6). The Lord has also promised
to "fulfill the desire of those that fear Him, and will
hear the desire of the humble." So that by these
promises it appears that hungering and thirsting, and
desires after grace, *are* grace in God's account and acceptance.

They are supernatural desires. It is true, there are
natural desires in the soul after that which is good. It is
the language of nature: "Who will show us any good?"
Now these desires may and do arise from the motion of
the natural and unsanctified will of man; and these desires are after happiness and not after holiness. Such

were the desires of Balaam, who said, "Let me die the death of the righteous, and let my last end be like his." This was a natural desire. But true desires in the soul are after heaven for holiness' sake. Bernard notably sets out the desires of natural men: "They have only a desire of the end and not of the means."

Desires after grace are joined with holy endeavors; and therefore the Apostle joins desire and zeal together to intimate that true desires are always joined with zealous endeavors. Thus the Apostle also joined a readiness of will and performance together. God will never accept the will for the deed unless there is an endeavor to perform what we say we are willing to do. And therefore Solomon rightly described how pernicious desires are without endeavors. "The desire of the slothful killeth him, because his hands refuse to labor." Bernard described this laziness of life: "Carnal men love to obtain, but love not to follow Christ; they will not endeavor to seek Him whom they desire to find."

Desires which are true and gracious are unsatisfiable. Thus David speaks of his desires: "My soul breaketh for the longing it hath to Thy judgments at all times." Yea, he further described the ardor and insatiableness of his desires by the "hart panting after the water brooks" (Psalm 42:1). The hart is naturally the most thirsty of all creatures, but this thirst is much increased when the poor beast is chafed with dogs. Even so, the true desires of the soul after grace are earnest, ardent, and vehement desires.

You may know true desires after grace by their object. Desires are not gracious if they are more after outward things than after God. So David: "My soul thirsteth after God, after the living God. My soul thirsteth for Thee, my flesh longeth after Thee, in a dry and thirsty land where no water is" (Psalm 42:2 and 63:1). Thus his soul longed and broke with longing after God's judgments. Now therefore, would you know whether you have any beginnings of grace in your soul? Then examine what your desires are. Perhaps you cannot pray, but do you desire to pray? Perhaps you cannot mourn, but do you desire to mourn? Perhaps you do not believe (as you fear), but do you desire to believe? Perhaps you cannot repent, but do you desire to repent? And do you labor to repent? Then you may conclude that you have some beginnings of true grace in your soul.

We may know the truth of grace, though it is little, by the earnest desire after the Word and means of grace. Thus Peter sets forth our desires: "as newborn babes, desire the sincere milk of the word, that ye may grow thereby" (1 Peter 2:2). There is in a child a natural instinct, as soon as ever born, to desire the mother's breast. The Apostle makes it a resemblance of a spiritual man: a man spiritually newborn will desire the Word and the means of grace that he may grow in grace.

We may know the truth of grace if we have an endeared love toward those who have grace. "By this we know we are passed from death to life, because we love the brethren" (1 John 3:14). Casuists, upon this text, say that love to God's children is the first grace, and first appears in young converts. The natives in New England, it is observed, upon their conversion (for God has begun there to bring some of those poor creatures "from darkness to light, and from the power of Satan to Himself"), show the first appearance of grace is in their love and respect to those who are truly gracious.

Thus I have shown you an answer to the question of what are the least measures of grace, without which (or at least some of which) a man cannot be said to have grace. And wherever any of these are, that man's condition is safe, and these little measures of grace will bring a man to heaven.

I shall here lay down some cautions to prevent misapplication.

CAUTION 1. Though those small measures of grace are saving, yet you must not content yourselves within them. Take heed, lest what I said for the support of the weakness of some Christians becomes not a pillow for the idleness of others. "But let us strive to go on unto perfection." We must not sit down with any measure of grace. And to persuade you hereunto:

Consider that things merely necessary and sufficient to maintain a natural life will not content a man. What man is content, though he has clothes enough to hide his nakedness, and food enough to keep his life and soul together? But he desires not only food for hunger and necessity, but delight. Now, shall men be unbound after their desires for outward things, and shall they sit down and say they have enough for heavenly things?

Consider, if you content yourself with a small measure of grace, though you shall have the fruit of your grace when you die, yet you will want the comfort of your grace while you live. It is strength of grace that gives assurance. Weak grace will bring your soul to heaven, but it is the strength of grace that will bring heaven into your soul. The work of righteousness shall be peace, and the effect of righteousness shall be quietness and assurance forever. A child of God seldom has peace and comfort from the habit of righteousness, but from the exercise of righteousness. "He that lacketh these things is blinded, and cannot see afar off" (2 Peter 1:9). This is not spoken of wicked men who have no grace, but of such as have grace; and because they exercise it not, they do not discern the comfortable fruits of grace in their souls. A little faith unexercised is, as to comfort (as we have shown), as good as no faith. They who add not to the stock of grace will want the comfort of grace. So that a weak Christian, who is compared by Peter to a blind man, cannot see (because the eyesight of his faith is weak) afar off; he cannot see his name written in heaven. He will want the comfortable evidence of grace in his heart who contents himself with small measures of grace.

CAUTION 2. Take not those things to be evidence of the truth of grace which are evidences only of the growth and strength of grace. Weak converts involve themselves in a labyrinth of misery in judging themselves by those symptoms which are evidences only of the strength of grace. You must not judge whether you are in the state of grace by whether you have ravishing joys and comforts of the Holy Ghost; these are things that God indulges unto some few, and those of a long standing in the school of Christ. In a school, a scholar must not compare himself with one of the highest form. If you would judge the truth of your grace, judge by the lowest measure.

The reason why hypocrites and weaker Christians err is this: hypocrites judge they have grace because

they have gifts, and weak Christians judge they have no
grace because they do not find such measures of grace
in them as in others. We do not usually say that it is not
day because it is not noon. It is unthankfulness to God,
and uncharitableness to ourselves, to argue a nullity of
grace from the weakness of it; and therefore if you
cannot say, "I see my grace," yet it is well if you can say,
"Blessed be God, I see my sin." If you cannot say that
you leave sin, yet it is well if you can say, "I have a full
purpose of heart to do so." If you can but cry out for
the want of grace, yet comfort yourself, and do not
conclude you have no grace.

Do not conclude you have small measures of grace
because you have but small measures of comfort. This
is the fault of young converts: they measure their grace
by their comfort, which is a false and deceitful rule.
Growth of grace is not to be measured by the working
of joy. The sweet blossom of joy may fall off when the
fruit of grace may come on. Yea, Christians of the
greatest measure of grace may have the least measure
of comfort, and all to let us know that as the being and
exercise, so the comforts of our graces come from free
grace. Our Lord Jesus Christ, who was anointed above
His fellows, and was full of grace and truth, yet in the
time of His desertion was without comfort when, by
reason of the suspension of the favor of God His
Father, He cried out, "My God, My God, why hast
Thou forsaken Me?"

And so, sometimes, Christians who have but little
measure of grace may have much comfort; and this is
the reason for that flash of joy that young converts
have. It is God's indulgence towards them to give them
great joy at their conversion; and indeed, their joy at

that time is more taken notice of because usually such have much trouble of mind when they pass through the pangs of the new birth. The change is then specific, which afterwards is but gradual. And so, though they have afterwards more grace, more settled joys and comforts, yet at their conversion they may have more sense of their joys, though afterwards they may find an increase of grace, when joy may be as real, though not as sensible. Therefore, do not judge your grace by your comforts.

Do not conclude that the measure of your grace is little because you have but a little measure of gifts. Gifts are the issues of time and experience, and the fruits of studies advantaged by the strength of natural parts. A man may have a quick and pregnant invention, a profound judgment, a retentive memory, a clear elocution, and the like, and yet none of these can be arguments of grace; all are but natural endowments. Gifts may be high and grace may be low. Thus it was with the church of Corinth: they were enriched with utterance and knowledge, and they came behind other churches in no gift, and yet the Apostle said of these very Corinthians that they were very low in grace; for so he charged them (1 Corinthians 3:1), that they were not spiritual, but carnal men, babes in Christ by reason of their envying, strife and divisions. They were carnal, and walked as men. Thus the church of Laodicea was rich and increased in gifts, and grew proud of it too, and yet for grace was poor, and naked, and blind, and miserable.

It is with some professors as it was with a well-read scholar who, having read many books of geography and description of places, could discourse of them very well; but if he were to travel to those countries of which he has so often read, he would soon be at a loss. So gifts may carry men far for matter of discourse about religion, but it is only grace that enables a man to practice religion. A child of God who has but little measure of gifts may have, for all that, much grace. Of all the seven churches of Asia, it is said of Philadelphia that she had but "a little strength" (Revelation 3:8), that is, but little strength of parts and gifts; and yet that church was very eminent for grace. For she had as much if not more faithfulness than the other churches, kept the word of Christ's patience, and did not deny His name. Judge not therefore your grace by your gifts. It is good to covet earnestly the best gifts, but the way of true grace (though but weak) is a more excellent way.

I shall conclude this point with some further consolation to the people of God who have but weak measures of grace.

Though you are but weak in yourself, yet you have much strength from without you, or rather it is in you because of the Spirit of Christ that dwells in your hearts, who believe the devil does all he can to make a little faith fail. But Christ prayed that it fail not. Great are the confederacies of the world, the flesh and the devil, against your little grace, but be of good comfort: "Ye are of God, little children, and have overcome them, because greater is He that is in you, than he that is in the world" (1 John 4:4). The weaker you are, the more advantage God has to magnify the glory of His power in your weakness.

Comfort yourselves, you weak Christians, for you have a strong God. In Jehovah is everlasting strength.

Your God is able to keep you from falling, and to present you faultless before the presence of His glory with exceeding joy. He is able by His almighty power through faith to keep you unto salvation. You have a strong God; fear not, His power will be magnified in your weakness.

You have a strong Savior. Though your grace is weak, yet He is able to save them to the uttermost that come unto God by Him. Christ is the wisdom and power of God to those who are called; yea, He is a strong Redeemer. "Our Redeemer is strong, the Lord of Hosts is His name" (Jeremiah 50:34). Satan is indeed the prince of the power of the air, for so he is called in Ephesians 2:2, but Jesus Christ is truly the great power of God, who is able, because stronger than the man armed, to bruise Satan under the feet of His saints.

You lie under a strong Word, which is able to carry on the work of grace begun in you. The Word of God, though it is foolishness to those who perish, yet it is the power of God to those who are saved; yea, it is an engine, "mighty through God to the pulling down of strongholds, casting down imaginations, and every high thing that exalts itself against the knowledge of God, and bringing into captivity every thought to the obedience of Christ" (2 Corinthians 10:4–5). Therefore the Apostle prays, "Now, brethren, I commend you to God, and to the word of His inheritance amongst all them that are sanctified." So cheer up; though faith is weak, yet the Word of God is strong. It is that ingrafted Word which is able to save your souls; yea, in a word, the Word of God is "profitable for doctrine, for reproof, for correction, for instruction in righteousness, that the man of God may be perfect, and thoroughly furnished unto all good works" (2 Timothy 3:16–17).

You are weak, but you stand on a sure foundation. It is a foundation; it is a sure foundation; it is the foundation of God. And it is the foundation of God that cannot shake, but stands firm. Now the weak believer stands by the immutable decree of God, which the Apostle calls the foundation of God (2 Timothy 2:19).

Weak believers are assisted by a strong Spirit. The Spirit of God is not only a Spirit of grace and supplication, but it is also a Spirit of power. And, therefore, let weak believers cheer themselves up; though they have but little grace, yet that little grace is upheld and maintained by the great power of God unto salvation.

The truth and essence of grace are not discerned so much by good acts as by good affections. "How fair is my love, my sister," said Christ to the spouse (Song of Solomon 4:10). God reckons our beauty by our love, and our perfection by the sincerity of our affections. Natural abilities, to which formalists and hypocrites may come up, may and do resemble good actions, but they cannot come up to good affections. A painter may paint the color of the face, but his art cannot give heat to the picture. Good actions may give you the resemblance of a Christian—as what Jehu did resembled a true reformer—but it is good affections that set out the life and heat of true grace. Judge your grace, therefore, by your affections, and take comfort in this: though you are little and low in actions, if you are warm in your affections, yours is true grace.

The third and last comfort is this: little grace shall

be lasting grace. Adam had perfection, but not perseverance; and you, poor soul, have imperfection of grace, but perseverance in grace. The most violent and impetuous flood of corruption shall not quench the least measure, the least spark of true grace. The most boisterous blast of temptation shall not extinguish this poor smoking flax; not one drop of this divine ointment shall be spilled as the water upon the ground. Comets may blaze a while and then they fall, to show that it was a comet and not a star. True stars do not, cannot fall. Oh, then, bless God, who though in His anger He "breaks the nations like a potter's vessel with an iron mace," yet such is His tenderness over weak believers that "He will not break the bruised reed" (Matthew 12:20). And though He puts out the candle of the wicked, yet "He will not quench the smoking flax."

The seeming graces of hypocrites shall perish and come to nothing, while true grace shall hold out. The painted face decays soon, but the natural complexion lasts. A child of God may be tossed by reason of corruption and temptation in a troublesome sea, but that ship shall never be shipwrecked whereof Christ is the pilot, the Scriptures the compass, the promises the tacklings, hope the anchor, faith the cable, the Holy Ghost the winds, and holy affections the sails, which are filled thus with the gales of the Spirit. "Fear not, therefore, little flock; for it is your Father's pleasure to give you the kingdom" (Luke 12:32).

Sermon 5

"Because in him there is found some good thing toward the Lord God of Israel, in the house of Jeroboam." 1 Kings 14:13

Having finished the former part of the doctrine about little measures of grace, I now come to the second part: God exactly takes notice of, tenderly cherishes, and graciously rewards the least beginnings and the smallest measures of grace in the hearts of His people.

In the prosecution of this point, I shall proceed in this method. I shall prove the truth of it, and I will also endeavor to give you the grounds hereof, and then make application.

First, that God thus cherishes the small beginnings of grace will appear if we consider:

1. These Scripture instances. Matthew 12:20: "He will not quench the smoking flax," that is, as I have shown already, He will kindle it. "He will not break the bruised reed," that is, He will strengthen it. God regards not the flame only, but the smoking of grace; not the ripe fruit, but the tender buds. Christ would have accepted green figs off the fig tree, though the time of ripe fruits was not yet come; so some expound Mark 11:13. Christ accepts not only the honey, but the honeycomb too, that is, say expositors, not only the excellent services, but even the meaner services of His people. God takes notice of the cries of our heart, even

the desires of the humble, even the most inward groanings of the soul; not a good word but God takes notice of it. Nay, God not only takes notice of the least good that is in His people, but He eyes also the common good that is in such as have no grace. Thus when the young man came to Christ, though he had no true grace, yet it is said "Jesus loved him." And He took notice of that discreet answer of the scribe, mentioned by Saint Mark, "and said unto him, 'Thou art not far from the kingdom of heaven' " (Mark 12:34).

2. The truth of this point may be made out by those sweet and gracious promises God has made to grace, though weak. I will give you one instead of many, mentioned by the prophet Isaiah: "He shall feed His flock like a shepherd, He shall gather the lambs with His arm, and carry them in His bosom, and gently lead those that are with young" (Isaiah 40:11).

3. By counsels that Christ gives to us, how we ourselves should carry ourselves to those who are weak, to use them with all tenderness. Now if God would have others do thus, then surely He Himself will deal with weak believers with much tenderness.

God would have the strong to bear with the weak, to bear with their infirmities, and not to please ourselves; and surely then God will bear with, and forbear them. See Psalm 103.

We are to receive them into our fellowship. "Him that is weak in the faith, receive you." And surely God will not reject such out of communion with Himself and His Son.

We must do nothing that will or may justly offend the weak. We must not walk uncharitably, and grieve our brother with our "meat." We must not make him stumble who is weak.

We should restore a weak brother who is fallen and put him in joint again. With the spirit of meekness, you that are spiritual, that is, strong Christians, help up such as are fallen through weakness.

We must strengthen the weak hands and confirm the feeble knees, and say to those who are of a fearful heart, "Be strong." We must help to lift up hands that hang down, and strengthen the feeble knees, lest that which is lame be turned out of the way, but rather that it be healed. We must not be like the herd of deer who push away from the poor wounded deer, but we must endeavor the healing of the wounded, and comfort the feeble-minded, and support the weak, and be patient towards all men; support the weak, i.e., set your shoulders to bear them up who would stand but are weak. Hold them up as a crutch does a body that is lame; help him to stand who is for weariness likely to fall. Let your charity help to hold them up, even as a beam holds up a house that is ready to fall. Now if God enjoins us to have all this care of those who are weak in grace—to cherish, support, and comfort them—then surely the God of mercy and compassion will be very careful to cherish the smallest measure of grace in the weakest believers.

QUESTION. Why does God cherish the least measures of grace in His people?

ANSWER. Because the least measure of grace is of a very great value; the least grace, and least measure or degree of it, is the purchase of Christ's blood and the merit of His great sufferings. The smallest spark of a diamond is precious; pearls and precious stones are but little for quantity, but great for quality and esteem. The least degree of grace is the work of God, and God will not forsake His own work.

Little grace is of the same nature and excellency with the greatest degree of grace, for as the very fillings of gold are of the same nature with gold, so the least measure of grace is grace. The faith of all believers is the same faith specifically, though not the same gradually; their faith is in all cases equally precious, but not equally strong.

God is the author of weak grace as well as of strong. Solomon gives a good rule why the rich should not slight the poor: "because God is the author and maker of them both." And God will not slight the poor in spirit any more than those who are rich in grace, for He is the maker of them both. It is an argument to us why we should not despise the poor: because God made him. And therefore, surely much more, because the Lord made the poor and weak Christian, He will not despise them.

Job said he did not despise the cause of his man-servant or maid-servant, and he gave a reason for it in Job 31:15: "Did not He that made me in the womb make him, and did not He fashion us in the womb?" which holds as a very firm argument why the rich should not despise the poor, and why the rich in grace should not despise those who are poor in grace: for God made and fashioned them both. Now what is a reason unto us, God is also pleased to make a reason unto Himself, that He will not forsake what He has formed, for so the prophet Isaiah said, "The Lord that created thee, O Jacob, and He that formed thee, O Israel, fear not; for I have redeemed thee, I have called

thee by thy name, for thou art Mine" (Isaiah 43:1).
And again, "Thus saith the Lord that made thee and
formed thee from the womb, 'Fear not, O Jacob my
servant, and thou Jeshurun whom I have chosen' "
(Isaiah 44:2). Yea, though Jacob is the worm, yet God
who made him will not crush him but cherish him.

See a gracious promise made to those who have but
little grace, upon the very ground that God is the author of the little grace. "Thy people also shall be all
righteous, they shall inherit the land for ever, the
branch of My planting, the work of My hand, that I
may be glorified. A little one shall become a thousand,
and a small one a strong nation; I the Lord will hasten
it in My time" (Isaiah 60:21–22).

The Lord will perfect His work which concerns His
people, i.e., He will perfect and encourage the least
beginnings of grace because grace is His work in His
servants. It is a very good argument in prayer: "O Lord,
forsake not the work of Thy hands." And though, in respect of outward things, God may destroy him whom
His hands have made and fashioned, it is otherwise in
respect of grace. God will not destroy any measure of
grace, which is the work of His hands. Property is the
ground of love, care and tenderness—as a man will
look to a weak child because it is his child, and will
repair a weak house because it is the house wherein he
dwells. And that is the third demonstration of God's
tender care over His people, that the meanest measure
of grace shall not be deserted or forsaken because God
is the author of it.

4. A fourth reason may be drawn from the covenant
of grace, the nature and tenor whereof is to accept sincerity instead of perfection, desires for deeds, purposes

for performances, pence for pounds, and mites for millions. Therefore God will accept and reward the least measure of grace that is in truth and sincerity. God required of Abraham, when He renewed with him the covenant of grace, "Be thou perfect (i.e., upright) and walk so before Me, and I will be thy exceeding great reward."

APPLICATION. To make some application of this truth, we may from hence deduce these inferences following. If God cherishes and will reward the smallest measure of grace, then it will follow that God takes notice of the smallest sins to punish them. He who graciously eyes the very budding of grace will also justly eye the budding of corruption in His own people. Thus He was ready to have slain Moses for his neglect of circumcising his son; and thus the Lord made a breach upon Uzzah when he put forth his hand and stayed the shaking of the ark. "You have I known (said God of His people), you only of all the families of the earth; therefore I will punish you for all your iniquities." It is true, it is said, "the Lord beholds not iniquity in Jacob, neither sees perverseness in Israel" (Numbers 23:21). But this is not as the antinomians interpret it, as if God did not see sin in His people so as eternally to punish it. And moreover, the most proper sense of that place is that whereas Balak hired Balaam to curse the people of Israel, and that false prophet, for the wages of unrighteousness, was ready enough to have taken all occasions of cursing them, yet he could not fasten any curse upon them at that time because there was no provoking sin among them. Therefore he gave Balak counsel to tempt them to sin, and so by the stumbling block of the Midianite women he drew Israel to idolatry and adultery, and so made them fall. But God does see sin in His own people, yea, the least sin; yea, He eyes their very failings, not to damn them for them, yet to chastise them for them. God sees the purposes of sin as well as the purposes of grace. It is said of Balak that he arose and warred against Israel (Joshua 24:9). Now we do not read that ever Balak actually waged war against Israel, only he intended and purposed it, and for that end sent and called Balaam the son of Beor to curse them. And yet the Holy Ghost reckoned upon his wicked purpose, as if he had accomplished it.

Learn from hence that the same mind should be in Christians of greater growth to the weak as was in Christ Jesus. Though He is higher than the highest, yet He looks upon the poor and lowly without disdain, and so should we. "The heaven is the throne, and the earth is the footstool of the Lord," and yet this great God will not despise the weakest saint, but "will look even to him that is poor, and of a contrite spirit, and trembleth at His word."

He will look on the poor, weak, trembling soul, and shall we look away from such with pride and disdain, and set such at our footstool? Shall Christ give the lamb in His scutcheon, and will you give the lion? Shall He, like a lamb, be meek and gentle, and you like the lion be stout, haughty, and stately, who condemns all the beasts of the forest? Oh, be not supercilious and contemptuous towards weak Christians, who are injured and discouraged by strong Christians:

1. When they are put upon such austerities of religion as are far beyond their strength and growth.

When these poor, torn, tattered, and rent bottles are put upon to hold new wine, alas, poor souls, they are discouraged; wherefore Christ proportions His doctrine to their capacities and will not say that to them which they cannot at present bear, and does not outmatch their strength with His commands. Fasting and suffering was a hard duty, and therefore He excuses them till they have more grace; which is a good rule for us, not to discourage young beginners in the school of Christ, not to put them to read such authors as are above their capacities.

2. When strong Christians are too sharp and rigorous in bitter reproofs for the failings and infirmities of weak Christians. Young converts, like young twigs, must be gently handled, else you will break them. You must excuse their failings, hide their wants, commend their performances, cherish their forwardness, resolve their doubts, and bear their burdens, and by this gentleness bring them into a love of religion that they may not have a distaste for it as soon as they know it.

3. By setting light by their gifts. Alas, how soon is the smoking flax quenched by the oversuperciliousness of those who think themselves bright torches! How easily is the poor spark of grace trodden out by the foot of pride!

4. By puzzling them with doubtful disputes, contrary to that of the Apostle: "Him that is weak in the faith receive, but not unto doubtful disputations" (Romans 14:1).

5. By giving them ill example. Weak Christians are more apt to be led by example than by precept. When Peter, who was a pillar in the church, and a strong Christian, for fear of persecution forsook the Gentiles,

and separated and withdrew himself, then others of
the Jews (which in all likelihood were weak Christians)
dissembled also. Thus Paul argued to abstain from giving ill example about the eating of things offered to
idols: "If any man see thee which hast knowledge (i.e.,
who art a strong Christian) sit at meat in the idol's
temple, shall not the conscience of him that is weak be
emboldened to eat those things that are offered to
idols?" (1 Corinthians 8:10).

And therefore, let Christians learn from God to
cherish the weak beginnings of grace in the people of
God. "Look not on me," said the church, "because I
am black, because the sun hath looked upon me"
(Song of Solomon 1:6), i.e., look not on me with a lofty
and disdainful look, and with a coy countenance. And
then the church adds, "my mother's children were
angry with me," that is, "other congregations and
people esteemed me low and disdained me for my
infirmity." But this should not be so among Christians,
but the strong should cherish the weak. Angels despise
not the poorest Christians, but minister unto them.

Learn from hence how God, by leisure and degrees, carries on in the hearts of His people the work
of grace unto further perfection. Mushrooms are such
worthless things, and like Jonah's gourd may spring up
in one night; but things of most moment are of long
growth before they come to perfection. The elephant
among the beasts, the oak among the trees, and man
among the rational creatures are longest before they
grow up to their full and perfect dimensions.

As it is in nature, so it is in grace: there is a progress
from less to greater; all this work is by degrees. The
godly are called "trees of righteousness," and yet this is

by degrees. There is first the budding forth of the earth, and then those things that are sown spring forth. And therefore let young converts learn from hence not to be discouraged. God's works, both of nature and grace, are perfected by degrees.

Though God regards the least measure of grace, let not this make you regardless to grow in grace. In the first creation God said to the creatures, "increase and multiply," and by virtue of that word the earth brings forth to this day. Now it is so in the new and second creation: the Lord expects that our grace should increase and multiply.

Though you have but a little grace, yet do not despise it or disparage it. Oh, do not despise the day of small things in your soul. Do not tread upon the bunch of grapes, upon the new wine in the cluster, but say, "there is a blessing in it." Do not despise a little grain of mustard seed; it will grow to a tree. True grace is a spark of heaven; do not tread it out. Despise not the least, and be not satisfied with the greatest measure of grace.

Let this comfort your poor soul, O weak Christian, whose burden it is that you have much corruption and but little grace. God will look over a great deal of sin and will take notice of the least grace. God will not, in refining His gold and silver, lose one dram of grace, though it lies among a heap of rubbish. Christ is said to have His fan in His hand. He will thoroughly purge His floor, and gather His wheat into His garner. Now the use of a fan is to cast out the worst, and keep in the best, to drive away the chaff of corruption; yet He will save and preserve every grain of grace. It is otherwise with the devil's sieve. Christ told Peter that Satan desired to sift him like wheat. Now the use of the sieve is contrary to the fan, for that keeps the worst and lets out the best. The devil does all he can to destroy our grace and increase our sin. But it is otherwise with God. He will kill your corruptions and cherish your graces, and if the least grace is in the soul, though with a mixture of much corruption, God will not despise it.

God carries the most tender regard to those who are weak in grace. The weak child is still carried in our arms, and the weakest of the flock the good Shepherd will carry in His bosom. Christ gave Peter charge in the first place to feed His lambs.

God's care over weak Christians is such that He will not suffer them to be tempted above what they are able, but with temptation will make a way to escape that they shall be able to bear it. God considers that we are but dust; and the wise Physician of our souls will mercifully weigh every grain of every dose, and will not outmatch their strength whose strength is small.

God will not put them on difficult duties at first. Christ taught His disciples such doctrines as their weakness could bear.

God will bear with their infirmities. He teaches His children to go, and holds them up by the arms.

Sermon 6

"Be strong in the grace of God, which is in Christ
Jesus." 2 Timothy 2:1

I have lately handled the doctrine of the small beginnings and the least measure of true grace, and have
shown you how God will accept and reward them, by
opening to you that passage in 1 Kings 14:13 concerning Jeroboam's son.

And lest that doctrine should accidentally (through
the corruption of our deceitful hearts) beget in us spiritual sloth, and satisfaction in weak degrees of grace,
therefore I shall prosecute my discourse concerning
the degrees of grace and show you that though God
regards weak grace, yet we must all labor to obey this
apostolic injunction: "Be strong in the grace of God,
which is in Christ Jesus."

In the whole verse you have three parts:
1. A loving address: "My son."
2. A pressing exhortation: "Be strong in grace."
3. The introductory illative: "Therefore."

First, the address.
QUESTION. How could Timothy be Paul's son?
For his father was a Greek, but Paul was a Jew of the
tribe of Benjamin. Timothy then was not Paul's son in
the flesh, but in the faith.

Now a further question is, why is he called Paul's
son?

Baldwin gives this reason: "Because Paul begat him to the faith," pointing to 1 Corinthians 4:17. Paul calls the Corinthians, whom he had converted to the faith, his beloved sons (verse 14), and so he calls Timothy in verse 17. But Timothy was not Paul's son in that sense, for, as Estius shows, he was converted long before Paul knew him by the godly instructions of his grandmother Lois and his mother Eunice.

The true reasons why Paul called Timothy his son were, first, because Paul was aged and Timothy young, and it was usual for the old to call the young sons; second, because he confirmed him in the faith; third, because he loved him as a son and Timothy loved Paul as a father; and, fourth, because as a son with his father, he served Paul in the gospel.

Before I come to the main doctrine, let me observe something in the passage to it: upon these reasons Paul calls Timothy his son. From the address, "My son" observe these things:

1. Ministers should use loving insinuations towards their hearers to usher in useful instructions. Soft words turn away wrath, and hard flints are broken upon soft pillows. This was Paul's practice here and elsewhere; he gained their affections the better to reform their judgment.

2. He calls him "my son" in relation to himself as a father. Observe that religion puts men into the nearest union and the most endeared relations. They who are glued together in the blood of Christ are knit together in the strongest bonds.

Now as for the reason of the duty—"therefore, my son"—expositors vary on what this illative particle "therefore" has reference to. Some, such as Estius, make it refer to verse 7 of the foregoing chapter: "God hath not given us the spirit of fear, but of power, of love, and of a sound mind." And if so, then observe that receiving the first degrees of grace should be a swaying reason to move us to grow in grace. Others refer it to Paul's example (verse 8) or to the example of Onesiphorus (verse 16). From whence may be observed that the good example of good men should be an argument to us to increase in goodness.

Or, if it refers to the 15th verse, "This thou knowest, that all they which are in Asia be turned away from me, of whom are Phygellus and Hermogenes" (as Theodoret refers it), then observe that other men's apostasy from the profession of grace should make the godly more careful to grow strong in grace.

But I shall handle the text without any relative considerations. "Be strong in the grace which is in Christ Jesus." Timothy may be considered in a double capacity, either as a minister or as a private Christian.

If as a minister, then the force of the exhortation lies in that he should increase in ministerial gifts and graces; whence may be observed that ministers of all men should grow in the truth and in ministerial gifts, because, as they grow, so will the people grow under their ministry. Ministers receive grace and apostleship for obedience to the faith among all nations (Romans 1:5). And grace is given unto them that they may "preach unto others the unsearchable riches of Christ" (Ephesians 3:8).

If he is considered as a private Christian, then he is exhorted not to content himself with grace received, but to labor after more strength of grace.

"Be strong in the grace which is in Christ Jesus."

Grace may be said to be in Christ in two ways, either as the subject recipient of grace, or as a fountain redundant and overflowing to His people. Grace is in Christ in all fullness, from whence His people receive grace for grace.

There are two observations which I shall note from the words considering the exhortation, without reference to what went before or follows after.

Believers are not to rest satisfied in weak measures of grace already received, but to endeavor to attain greater strength of grace.

Christ is the subject in which all grace is, and the fountain from which believers must receive all their grace.

In the opening of the first doctrine, the first thing is to make it appear that believers must not rest satisfied with weak measures of grace received, but must labor after more grace. This I shall prove by various instances:

The first instance is when believers have grown from weak grace to strong grace, "who out of weakness were made strong." There are expositors who refer this place to Hezekiah's recovery in 2 Kings 20. But it may have a more general extent and application. The psalmist spoke of God's people: "They go from strength to strength, every one of them in Zion appears before God" (Psalm 84:7). It is true, the proper reference of these words is to the Jews going up to Jerusalem to worship, when the males went thrice a year up to Jerusalem to worship, according to the law (Exodus 23:14–17). Yet [Henry] Ainsworth understands it of our growth in grace; so we are said to be changed from glory to glory, that is, from little degrees of grace to greater. Grace is but glory begun, and glory is but grace perfected. True grace is still aspiring unto perfection; and therefore Paul says, "if by any means I might attain the resurrection of the dead" (Philippians 3:11). His meaning is "that I may attain that perfection of holiness which accompanies the state of resurrection," a metonymy of the subject for the adjunct. He is still pressing forward that he might attain further degrees of grace, and for that end Paul forgot what was behind, and reached forth to those things that were before (verse 13). And though Paul (as he writes in Ephesians 3:4) had very great knowledge in the mystery of Christ, yet he still desired to know more and more of Christ. This requirement is made clear to us:

By instances wherein God's people have prayed for the strength of grace. "I bow my knees (said Paul) unto the Father of our Lord Jesus Christ, that He would grant unto you, according to the riches of His glory, to be strengthened with might by His Spirit in the inner man" (Ephesians 3:14–16). And speaking to the Romans (15:13) he says, "I am persuaded you are full of goodness and knowledge"; yet, because the best and most learned know but in part, and see but darkly through a glass (1 Corinthians 13:12), he prays that God would "fill them with all joy and peace in believing, that they might abound in hope through the power of the Holy Ghost." So he prayed that their "love might abound more and more in knowledge and in all judgment; and they might be filled with the knowledge of His will in all wisdom and spiritual understanding, that they might walk worthy of the Lord, unto all pleasing, and be fruitful in every good work, increasing in the knowledge of God."

Thus God's people have prayed for a further increase in grace. Paul, after his conversion, increased
more in strength, whereby he was enabled to confound
the opposing Jews at Damascus (Acts 9:22).

By commands. Leaving the first principles of the doctrine of Christ, we must go on to perfection; we must
be diligent to add grace to grace. We are commanded
to be strong in the Lord, to stand fast in the faith, to
acquit ourselves like men and be strong, and to
abound more and more. Many such commands are
scattered up and down the Scripture, which shows our
duty to grow more and more, and to attain unto
greater measure of grace.

By promises that God's people shall do so. "The path of
the just is as the shining light that shineth more and
more to the perfect day," that is, they shall increase
more and more in strength. God's gentleness makes
His people great, and enlarges their steps under them.
The feeble among them at that day shall be as David,
"and the house of David shall be as God, as the angel
of the Lord before them." Pareus, in his short notes,
which he calls his *Adversaria,* said, "He that is weak in
faith shall be as David, strong in faith."

Why should believers not rest satisfied with the first
beginnings of grace, but labor to be grown and strong
Christians?

The reason may be drawn partly from the necessity
of it: why you must do it; and partly from the danger of
it: if you do it not.

From the necessity of it, there are these reasons:

1. Consider the strong temptations you are likely to
meet with from the devil. We are therefore commanded to be strong in the Lord, to put on the whole

armor of God that we might be able to stand against the wiles of the devil. "For we wrestle not against flesh and blood, but against principalities and powers, and against the rulers of the darkness of this world" (Ephesians 6:12). Now, shall the devil be strong and armed, and shall we be content to be unarmed and weak Christians? Note 1 John 2:14: "I write unto you young men because ye are strong, and the word of God abideth in you, and you have overcome the wicked one." But when he writes to children he says, "I write unto you, because your sins are forgiven for His name's sake" (verse 12), intimating that though weak grace is sufficient to evidence to us the pardon of sin, yet it is strong grace that is able to overcome the temptations of the devil. The devil shall not overcome the weakest measure of grace; but the stronger our grace is, the more able we are to resist and overcome that enemy of our salvation. The devil is called a roaring lion whom we must resist, steadfast in the faith. It is not weak faith which is able to grapple with the devil; therefore we ought to be grown and strong Christians.

2. Consider the strong opposition we are likely to meet with from the world. We may be put upon, as Paul, to fight with beasts. Such manner of unreasonable men we may meet with, and therefore we are commanded to "watch and stand fast in the faith," to "quit ourselves like men and be strong" (1 Corinthians 16:13). And the reason is given in verse 9: there are many adversaries we are likely to meet with, and therefore we need to pray with the Psalmist to be "strengthened and saved by the right hand of the Lord" (Psalm 138:3, 7). Weak faith is not fit to be in a crown of opposition, and therefore we should labor to

grow strong in the grace of God.

3. We have many strong corruptions in our hearts which weak grace will never be able to mortify: strong passions and strong lusts. And how shall weak grace be able to grapple with and have a conquest over these? If your graces are weak when your corruptions are strong, you will be miserably followed by your corruptions. Therefore, pray for strengthening and assisting grace whereby you may be able not only to resist, but to subdue and mortify the strongest lusts and passions in your heart.

Another ground of the doctrine is taken from the danger: "if you grow not strong in grace."

1. Others who made profession of religion after you in time will go before you in measures and degrees of grace. So it is said, "Many that are first shall be last, and the last shall be first." Those who were first in the profession of the gospel shall be last in the degrees and measures of grace because they have not improved grace to a further increase of it.

2. If you do not grow strong in grace, you will be sure to decay and grow weaker. For to not go forward in grace is to go backward. Grace may be lost in some degree, and as to its exercise and comfort, though not to its being. Therefore the Apostle says, "If these things be in you and abound, they make you that ye shall neither be barren nor unfruitful" (2 Peter 1:8). This intimates that you will be barren if you do not add grace to grace. Weak things, if they are not watched over and strengthened, will be ready to die.

3. Though you cannot lose the being of your grace, yet you will lose the comfort of it; and you may be in as

much trouble and perplexity as if you had no grace at all. It's true, weak grace will bring your soul to heaven, but it's only strong grace that will bring heaven into your soul. Little grace is like a little mote which is not seen because it is little. Little grace is, as it were, no grace; that man in the gospel called his faith "unbelief": "Lord, help my unbelief" (Mark 9:24). Weakness of grace makes men's persuasions of God's love to be presumption, their zeal to be lukewarmness, their grace to be but gifts, and here their faith to be but unbelief.

It is strong grace which gives gladness of heart and hope in God. Without it, as Jeremiah said, "My strength and my hope is perished from the Lord" (Lamentations 3:18). When strength in grace decays, then hope and comfort decay also. It is the Apostle's prayer in the inscription of many of his epistles: "grace and peace be multiplied." If therefore you do not increase your graces, you will neither increase nor keep your comforts. "He that lacketh these things is blind, and cannot see afar off" (2 Peter 1:9). It is not meant of a total lack of grace (as has been shown), for, as afterwards is expressed, he is purged from his old sins, though he forgets it, having lost the sense of pardon for want of adding grace to grace.

4. Weak grace under great trials will expose a man to doubts and falls, as if he had no grace at all. Little grace will keep a man in small trials, but not in greater. Little grace, as to the straits a man may be in, may be as good as no grace; and therefore, when the disciples were at sea, and a great tempest arose insomuch that they were afraid, that which is said in Matthew to be little in Mark is said to be no faith. This intimates that, as

to that particular exigence and strait they were in, their little faith stood them in no more stead than if they had no faith at all. So Christ called Peter "O ye of little faith," because though he began to walk upon the waves, yet Matthew 14:30 says that "when the winds grew boisterous, he was afraid and began to sink." Peter did not sink into the sea before his faith began to sink in his soul. He who faints in the day of adversity argues that his strength is small; so said Solomon in Proverbs 24:10.

I should now proceed to a second particular, and that is to give some Scripture notes of that man who is grown in grace. But let me shut up this sermon with a just and sharp reproof of many professors in our time who go from one ordinance to another, and yet make little progress or increase in religion. They may be fitly compared to a company of ants who are very busy about a molehill, and run to and fro but never grow great. Even so we have many Christians who run from one church to another, from one preacher to another, and, it may be, from one opinion to another, but never grow up in true grace and the true knowledge of Jesus Christ. But I shall meet with such people hereafter in this discourse.

Sermon 7

"Be strong in the grace of God, which is in Christ Jesus." 2 Timothy 2:1

I have, in the former chapter, observed from the apostolic injunction to Timothy that which is obligatory to all Christians: It is the duty of all believers not to rest satisfied in weak measures of grace which they have received, but they are to endeavor to attain unto greater strength of grace.

This point we have proved by Scripture instances, and also by several reasons. Now I proceed to answer to this question:

QUESTION. What are the notes the Scripture lays down of strong and grown Christians?

ANSWER. We are to know there are marks in Scripture, both of the truth of grace as well as the strength of grace, and these must not be confounded, but distinctly considered. Our present question is about marks of growth in grace.

1. Such as are grown in grace ordinarily enjoy a grounded assurance and comfortable manifestation of the love of God in Christ to their souls. So St. John said, "perfect love casteth out fear." The more perfect love is, the less of tormenting fear is in the soul; and the reason for our fear and doubting is want of love. We cannot comprehend the great love of God in Christ to our souls till we are "strengthened with might by His Spirit in the inner man," which you will see in

the Apostle's prayer for the Ephesians, "that God would grant unto them, according to the riches of His glory, to be strengthened with might by His Spirit; that Christ might dwell in their hearts by faith, and that they might be rooted and grounded in love; and that they might be able to comprehend with all saints what is the breadth, and length, and depth, and height, and to know the love of Christ" (Ephesians 3:16–19). So that the more strength of grace is in the soul, the clearer is our comprehension of Christ's love for the soul.

2. Strong and grown Christians are able, experimentally, to comfort others with the same comfort wherewith they themselves are comforted of God; and when they are converted they are able to strengthen their brethren, as Christ said to Peter. By conversion in that place is not meant the first work of grace in the soul, for that was wrought in Peter before his fall, but the meaning is: "Peter, when you are strengthened and recovered from your fall, when you have recovered your strength again, then see that you are careful to strengthen others, who perhaps may fall into the same weakness as yourself." "If any man be overtaken with a fault (said Paul to the Galatians in 6:1), you that are spiritual, restore such a man in the spirit of meekness." You who are spiritual, i.e., you who are grown and experienced Christians, see that you do all you can to recover such a fallen brother.

Paul prayed for the Philippians that their love "may yet abound more and more, in all knowledge with judgment" (1:9), that is, that they might have knowledge with judgment and experience so they might use their judicious knowledge in love for the edification of others who are but weak in grace. And in the epistle to the Romans, the same Apostle laid down this characteristic of a strong Christian: "I am persuaded of you my brethren, that you are full of goodness, filled with all knowledge, able also to admonish one another" (15:14), from whence we may gather the inference that the more perfect any Christian is in knowledge, or any other grace, the more able he is to admonish others, for their edification.

3. Grown Christians are such as understand the great and profound mysteries of religion. They are not only such as use milk, and understand only the first and plain principles, such as the Apostle calls "babes, and unskillful in the word of righteousness." But they are such as are able to digest strong meat, i.e., the deep mysteries of the gospel. They understand in some measure, and have their "senses exercised to discern both good and evil," that is, to judge between true doctrines and false. Strong and grown Christians have such an ear as is able to try words (as it is in Job 34:3) "even as the mouth trieth meats." It is an observation of the learned Mercer that the same word in Hebrew which signifies "ear" in the dual number signifies "a pair of balances," to note that an experienced and judicious Christian will weigh whatever he hears before he believes it. For as the tongue of the balance stands as a judge between the two scales, so should the heart of every man weigh what he hears, and so will every grown and judicious Christian. He will not take up truth upon trust, but he considers first and believes afterwards. Nor will a grown Christian be satisfied with inferior knowledge, but will, like a grown scholar, be searching after the deep things of God.

4. A grown, experienced, and strong Christian is most conversant and employed in the most strict and severe exercises of religion which tend most to mortification. Weak Christians are all for easy and ordinary exercises, such as hearing and reading good books, but a strong Christian is much in spiritual watchfulness, secret prayer, frequent fasting, self-denial, heavenly meditation, and such like duties as have a special influence upon the mortification of sin and corruption. A child whose parts and strength are weak is not conversant about such arduous and great undertakings as a grown man.

5. He can believe the accomplishment of promises and Scripture prophecies, though God's providence may seem to make against them, and though there seem no outward probabilities for them. Thus it argued that Abraham was strong in faith, who "against hope, believed in hope, and being not weak in faith, he considered not his own body now dead" (Romans 4:18–19). There were several things that might have staggered Abraham's faith, had it not been very strong:

There were fifteen years, at least, between the making of the promise of giving him a son and the fulfilling of it.

Abraham was about a hundred years old before he had a son, and so was unlikely to have children.

Sarah's womb was dead, with no ordinary hope of procreation.

And after the promised son was born, God called upon Abraham to offer him up; yet, notwithstanding all this, he "staggered not at the promise of God through unbelief, but was strong in faith, giving glory to God, and was fully persuaded, that what He had promised He was able also to perform" (Romans 4:20–21).

6. A strong believer can suffer as well as do for the sake of Christ. Greater strength of grace is required to suffer for the truth than to profess the truth; and therefore our Savior propounds this to the ambitious suitors, the sons of Zebedee: "Are ye able to drink of the cup that I shall drink of? and to be baptized with the baptism, wherewith I am baptized withal?" He implied that they did not well understand their own strength, that there was more grace required to suffer for the name of Christ than to believe on the name of Christ; and according as is our strength of grace, so is our courage for the cause of Christ less or more. Nicodemus, when he had but little grace, came to Jesus "but yet in the night," by stealth. He dared not openly appear for Christ; but afterwards, as he grew in grace and knowledge of Christ, so he grew courageous for Christ. And when the cause of Christ was debated in the assembly of the chief priests and Pharisees, there Nicodemus boldly pleaded the cause of Christ: "Does our law judge any man before it hears him, and knows what he does?" (John 7:51).

Nay, we read afterward of a higher resolution of this once fearful Nicodemus, when Christ was crucified and at the lowest. We find that Nicodemus, "who (says the text) came at first to Jesus by night, brought a hundred pound weight of mixture of myrrh and aloes, for the burial of Christ" (John 19:39). The like instances we have in Joseph of Arimathea, who was a disciple of Christ but secretly, for fear of the Jews. But afterwards, when he had more strength of grace, the Scripture tells us "he went in to Pilate boldly, and craved the body of Jesus." To profess Christ boldly, in a time when dangers and difficulties attend that profession, argues a strong faith. A weak constitution dares not go out unless the weather is fair, but a strong body can endure the hardest weather. A weak and young convert is more fit to live in prosperity of the gospel, but an old experienced Christian, like an old, tired soldier, will not shrink in the hardest trials. If you faint in the day of adversity, it is because "thy strength is small."

7. He is one who is able to govern his tongue; though passion is in the heart, yet through the strength of his grace he bridles it in and restrains it so that it shall not break into open railings, revilings, and clamors as others do. Saint James gives this characteristic of a strong Christian: "If any man offend not in word, the same is a perfect man" (James 3:2), not legally, but evangelically; he is a perfect man, i.e., he has grown strong in the grace of God.

8. He is one who dares trust God's providence for outward things, however he is in straits. As it argues littleness of faith to distrust Christ for food and raiment, so it argues strength of faith that, though the vision tarries and no deliverance appears, a man then lives by faith, as the just are said to do; this argues strength of faith.

9. He is one who labors for unity in the church as well as for purity in the church. He will labor, to the extent of his power, that Christ's coat shall be without rent as well as without spot. This characteristic I gather from the exhortation of the Apostle: "Let us therefore, as many as be perfect, be thus minded, and if in any thing ye be otherwise minded, God shall reveal even

this unto you. Nevertheless, whereto we have already attained, let us walk by the same rule, let us mind the same thing" (Philippians 3:15–16). It is a note you are weak when you make a stir in the church about your opinions. Weak children are most forward. When children are weak and sickly, nothing will please them; but a grown experienced Christian is sober and wise and very earnest to preserve unity in the church of Christ.

Before I proceed to speak any more about strength of grace, I shall make some applications of what I have delivered about the marks and signs of strong grace. And the use I shall make shall be to give you some cautions about these foregoing characteristics, and there is need of a twofold caution.

First, take heed that you do not imagine yourselves strong in grace when you are weak. This is a dangerous mistake.

Second, take heed of thinking and judging yourselves weak in grace when you are strong in grace; this is an uncomfortable mistake. "There is a man (said Solomon) that maketh himself rich, and hath nothing; and there is a man that maketh himself poor, and yet hath great riches." I would therefore caution you that you may neither live above nor beneath what you have, that you do not proudly fancy you have what you have not, nor discouragedly fear you want what you indeed have.

With regard to the first caution:

1. You are not to measure the strength of grace by the length of your profession. Many who are long standers in the profession of religion are but slow walkers in the ways and practice of religion. The soul's

proficiency in grace is not the issue of length of time, but the fruit of free grace. There were those in the church for so long a time that they ought to have been teachers of others, but they had attained but little growth in strength of grace. They who came at the eleventh hour had their penny as well as those who came early into the vineyard. The scope of this parable is (as some interpreters say) to show that those who come late to the profession of religion may yet outdo many in gifts and graces who have been long before them in profession. How many among us are there, with regard to whom their years speak them eighty, but their knowledge and grace not eighteen?

2. Measure not the strength of grace by the strength of your affections for some of the ways of God. The love of a newly married couple may be more zealous at first; afterwards it is more solid. Women, who are the weaker vessels, are usually more affectionate. Weak Christians are usually most affectionate. When the cripple was cured, we read that upon the first cure he leaped for joy. It is likely he did not continue to do so; the newness of the change much affected him, and so it does young converts.

3. Measure not the strength of grace by the abundance of the means of grace which you enjoy. Alas, Laodicea had a glorious light shining amid her. She was one of the seven candlesticks. And because she had such means of grace she mistook herself, saying, "I am rich, and increased with goods, and have need of nothing." But, said Christ, "thou knowest not that thou art wretched, and miserable, and poor, and blind, and naked" (Revelation 3:17).

4. Measure not the strength of grace by the

strength of your gifts. There is a new disease among children called the rickets, and this is when children grow big in the head but weak in their limbs. This disease is spiritually upon the souls of many of our poor professors; their heads grow in respect of gifts and knowledge, but they do not grow strong to walk in the ways of God. They are like the moon: increasing in light but not in heat. In the days of the schoolmen, the gifts of men were very high, and yet the power of godliness was at a low ebb; there were in those times many sublime notions, seraphic speculations, curious distinctions, subtle objections, and elaborate answers—to them, grave and weighty sentences. But alas, there was but a little of the power of grace in the hearts of those men and those they taught.

The second caution is to prevent mistakes of those who are apt to judge themselves weak in grace when indeed they are strong in grace.

1. Because you have not perfection of grace, do not therefore conclude you have no strength of grace. Truth of grace is one thing, and strength of grace is another; so strength of grace is one thing, and perfection of grace is another. You must wait for perfection till you come to heaven; it is there only where the spirits of just men are made perfect. It is a witty observation someone has made: in grammar, the present tense is accompanied with the imperfect tense. Even such is our present state of grace: it is accompanied with imperfections; but our future shall be more than perfect. There is no perfection here: "there is not a just man upon earth that doth good and sinneth not," said Solomon. Who can say, "I have made my heart clean?"

"If I wash my hands with snow water (said Job), and make myself ever so clean, yet shalt thou plunge me in the ditch, and my own clothes shall abhor me." That is, though I have by regeneration some grace, yet all my defilements shall never in this life be put away.

In the prophecy of Zechariah, we have the Lord speaking thus: "I will refine them as silver, and try them as gold is tried." And yet in the prophet Isaiah God said, "I have refined thee, but not with silver." To reconcile both places, the meaning is that though God begins to refine His people, yet they are not perfectly refined.

2. Do not judge yourself weak in grace because you do not have not strong affections. God makes up in the experience of old, grown Christians what is wanting of the great affections they had at their first conversion. Holy Greenham often prayed that he might keep up his young zeal with his old discretion. What is wanting in affections, God makes up to you in solidity of judgment, cleanness of knowledge, abundance of experience, and stableness in the faith.

3. Judge not the strength of your grace by the strength of your comforts; the fruit may grow strong when the blossom is off. I have spoken of this before, and therefore will only add this: heavenly joys and raptures are very sparingly found among God's people. They are God's special indulgences to some of His special children. I will conclude with a saying of a godly and learned Scotchman: "While I live, I never expect to see a perfect reformation in the church or feel perfect, ravishing joys in my heart."

Sermon 8

"Be strong in the grace of God, which is in Christ Jesus." 2 Timothy 2:1

CASE 1. Are strong temptations consistent with strong grace? This is a needful and practical case, because the people of God, when tempted by the devil, not only question the strength but the truth of their grace.

Before I resolve this case, I shall premise these general positions.

1. It is certain, where there is truth of grace there may be strong temptations from the devil. The devil is like a thief who robs not outhouses, where there is nothing but dung and straw, but the cabinets that are in the closet. So this great thief of the world is not so eager to rob and spoil the outhouses—wicked and ungodly men—but those who have riches of grace in the cabinets of their hearts; not upon an empty vessel, but upon a ship laden with rich merchandise. Those who are fraught with the rich gifts of grace, the devil, by his temptations, will labor to make a prize of for himself.

2. Let the temptations of the devil be never so strong, yet they shall not be above the strength of grace which believers have received from God. "God is faithful, who will not suffer you to be tempted above that you are able" (1 Corinthians 10:13). He will proportion the burden to the back, and the stroke to the strength of him who is to bear it; if temptations increase, our

strength shall also increase whereby we may be able to grapple with them.

3. It is evident that the temptations of the devil are always, ordinarily, most strong after God's people have discharged some extraordinary duties to God, or have received most discoveries of grace from God. In both these cases the devil's temptations are usually great. You find that immediately after the celebration of the Lord's Supper, the devil desired to winnow the disciples. After they had performed that extraordinary service to God, the devil was desirous presently to set upon them. So you find that after Christ had in an extraordinary manner fasted forty days and forty nights, He was immediately tempted by the devil. And so also, no sooner was He out of the water of baptism but He was in the fire of temptation.

The Israel of God can be no sooner out of Egypt, but this hellish Pharaoh pursues them. Hezekiah had no sooner kept the solemn Passover, but Sennacherib came up against him. All this is to show us that after we have put forth most grace in a duty, then the devil will labor to play his after-game with us if he misses with his fore-game. If Satan cannot keep us from duty, and from enlargement in duty, he will pierce our duties with pride and so mar them. And so, after we have received the most especial manifestation of God's love and favor in Christ, then may we expect to be assaulted by the devil.

After Paul had those heavenly raptures and abundance of revelations, the devil set upon him with vile temptations. He had the messenger of Satan to buffet him, "a thorn in the flesh," which is not meant of any disease, but some sharp temptation from the devil. So you find that immediately after the voice to Christ said, "This is my beloved Son, in whom I am well pleased," then the tempter came to Him. You may gather the same from that connection between those two petitions in the Lord's Prayer: "forgive us our trespasses," and "lead us not into temptation," to note to us that no sooner can we get the evidence of our pardon but we may expect to be tempted of the devil.

4. Men who have the greatest strength of grace are likely to meet with the fiercest assaults and strongest temptations from the devil. And this brings me to answer the original question: are strong temptations consistent with strong grace?

ANSWER. To clarify and confirm this, there are these two particulars to be inquired into:

When may temptations be said to be strong?

How and why such strong temptations may be consistent with strong grace.

QUESTION 1. Now to deal with the first particular: when may temptations be said to be strong?

Temptations may be said to be strong when the solicitations of the devil to sin are urgent with the soul; when they are not weak and faint suggestions, but violent assaults which will not be removed until assented to; when the devil haunts a man so that he will not let him alone; then may they be said to be strong. Thus it is said in 1 Chronicles 21:1, "Satan stood up against Israel," i.e., he set himself to tempt David "and provoked him." He would not let him alone, but haunted him with hellish importunity "till he had numbered the people."

Temptations may be said to be strong when they are frequent and continued. Small temptations often suggested become strong ones. Small drops of water by frequent falling make hollow the hard stone, which a few great and forcible blows will not do. So temptations, though but to small sins, if they are continued, may have greater entrance into the heart than a violent assault may.

Temptations may be said to be strong when they are suited by the devil to a man's disposition or present condition. So was that temptation by which the devil set upon Christ after He had fasted forty days and forty nights: "Command that these stones be made bread." It was suited to His present condition: meat for His hunger. If you offer meat to a naked man or clothes to a hungry man, he values it not, because it is not suited to the man's necessity; but if you offer clothes to him who is naked, and meat to him who is hungry, then it becomes acceptable.

The devil does not cast temptations at random; he is more subtle than to row against wind and tide; he knows which way the stream of our affections and dispositions runs, and suits his baits accordingly. "Every man is tempted when he is drawn away of his own lust and enticed" (James 1:14). It is a metaphor taken from fishermen who have this skill: according to the nature of the fish will they suit their bait, whereby they lie in wait to deceive either the sight or taste of the poor fish. The devil is the great fisher of souls, and makes use of such temptations as are most likely to take hold. He observes to what sins a man's relations, calling, or opportunities lay him most open and vulnerable and accordingly lays his snare and spreads his net. Though it is true that every man has a principle within him suiting to every sin, yet it is as true that every man is not equally active for or disposed to every sin. The devil sees what sin is most predominate in man, and so he frames his temptations suitably. He sets a wedge of gold before a covetous Achan; Cozbi, a harlot, before an adulterous Zimri; a fair preferment before an ambitious Absalom. He knows well that a fit object presented is a victory half obtained. In these three cases temptations may be said to be strong.

QUESTION 2. How does it appear that temptations so urgent, so continued, and so suited may be consistent with strong grace?

ANSWER 1. By instances whereby it appears the best of God's children have been most tempted. Job was a holy man, yet with what strong temptations was he assaulted! The devil impoverished him in his estate, and so would tempt him to distrust God's providence. He took away the lives of all his children to make him question providence; he tormented him with grievous diseases to make him clamor against providence, and above all this tempted him to "curse God and die," by the instigation of his wife. And yet, though Job was thus haunted by evil, he was a believer strong in grace, and the most eminent saint in that age and that part of the world at that time, as God himself testified that there was "none like him upon earth, a perfect and an upright man" (Job 1:8). He was not only for riches the greatest of all the men of the east, but for holiness the greatest upon the earth; yet thus was he afflicted and assaulted by the devil.

Another instance is David, an eminent believer. He has this commendation, that he was "a man after God's own heart." And yet how furiously was he tempted by the devil! One temptation was when Satan moved him to number the people, another was to defile another man's wife, another was to counterfeit himself as mad before Achish king of Gath, another was to judge all his holy duties to be in vain, and at another time to question the faithfulness of God in His promise to make him king. He said in his haste that "all men were liars" (Psalm 116:11), even Samuel the prophet also. Thus Peter was an eminent apostle of Christ, after he had made such a glorious confession of his faith, and had discovered more grace than in all his lifetime before, you find him suddenly, by an instigation from the devil, beginning to rebuke Christ, and counseling Him to spare Himself.

Thus Paul, who had such high and heavenly raptures, such divine ecstasies, yet had the messenger of Satan to buffet him. But above all instances you have Jesus Christ, who though He had perfect grace, and was full of grace and truth, yet this could not exempt Him from the temptations of the devil. He was full of the Holy Ghost, yet was He forty days tempted by the devil, and that with strong temptations, if you consider their continuance, their urgency one after another, and their suitability to His present condition. So it is plainly manifest that strong temptations may be consistent with strength of grace by these instances given.

It appears also by reasons drawn from God, for the clear illustration of the glory of His own attributes. And therefore the Scripture is clear in this, particularly to show how the temptations of God's people make His attributes to be more illustrious. First, by His faithfulness: "God, who is faithful, will not suffer you to be tempted above that you are able" (1 Corinthians 10:13). And then also hereby will His pity and compassion be made glorious. Therefore Christ "became like unto us, that He might be a merciful high priest, able to succor and pity those that are tempted" (Hebrews 2:17–18). And then, last, the glory of His power. In our weakness God will manifest His power, for His "strength is made perfect in weakness." Thus it pleases God to exercise His people with great afflictions and temptations for the setting out of His own glorious attributes, and magnifying of His own name.

ANSWER 2. Another reason may be drawn from God's people themselves.

God in afflicting His children aims at their good. Thus, when the devil tempted David to number the people, and when he was sacrificing at the floor of Ornan the Jebusite, there God told him that the temple should be built. This was the issue of his temptation. So when Job was so tempted and afflicted in the issue, all was for his good. Job's graces would never have been so illustrious, had not the devil's temptations been so furious. This is one end of God's afflicting His people, that their graces may become more radiant.

Another may be to check pride. There is no greater temptation in the world to pride than eminence in grace. Pride is that worst fruit which grows upon the best stock. 'Tis not so much the ornaments of the body as the endowments of the mind which stir up pride; and this was Paul's case. After his abundance of revelations, there was a thorn in his flesh, a messenger of Satan, to buffet him lest he should be lifted up. God will suffer those who have strong grace to be strongly tempted in order to check the pride of their hearts.

The godly are more able to grapple with strong temptations than weaker Christians are, and so God suits the service and sufferings of His people to the proportion of their strength of grace.

ANSWER 3. Another reason may be taken from the devil, from that malice which he bears to all the people of God. Especially those who have the most grace, whom God loves most, the devil hates most. When the voice from heaven said to Christ, "Thou art My well beloved Son," then came the devil to assault and to tempt Him. If you are the objects of God's dearest love, you will be the objects of the devil's deepest rage; and though he cannot damn your soul, yet he will bruise your heel.

It also proceeds from the devil's knowledge as well as malice. He knows if he can but get those who are strong in grace to sin, he shall do the more mischief. It will open the mouths of wicked men to blaspheme God and religion, as in the case of David: "By this deed thou hast given occasion to the enemies of the Lord to blaspheme." How were the mouths of God's enemies opened to blaspheme His name!

It will embolden the weak in sin with more freedom when they see those who are eminent fall. And thus the example of Peter made the Gentiles to "judaize." When the strong abuses his liberty, he becomes a stumbling block to those who are weak. When Phygellus and Hermogenes turned away from the faith, how did all Asia turn aside also! When men of eminent gifts apostatize, how do they draw others in abundance!

It will provoke God to inflict heavy judgments on

the places where you dwell. Thus the devil knew that if he could get David to number the people, it would procure a judgment upon them; and therefore it is not said that he stood up against David, but against Israel, "and provoked him to number the people." He well knew that if he could prevail with David, all Israel would suffer for it. Thus we see that where there is strength of grace, there may be and are strong temptations.

OBJECTION. But here may an objection be raised from 1 John, where it is said, "He that is born of God sinneth not, and keepeth himself that the wicked one toucheth him not" (5:18); and that they which are strong have overcome the wicked one. And if this be so, how can it be true that strong temptations from the devil may be consistent with strong grace in the heart?

ANSWER. When it is said that "the wicked one toucheth him not," it is not to be taken absolutely, as if the devil did not tempt a man at all; therefore there must be a restriction of the clause "he toucheth him not," that is, with a deadly touch. And so Cajetan said: "This phrase excludes not the kinds of temptations, but that we are not hurt, nor eternally destroyed by them." But I conceive rather that these words have a peculiar reference to the 16th verse, where mention is made of a sin unto death. The devil shall not prevail or touch a man so as to commit that sin which is unto death. Though he may tempt, and will be continually assaulting a man, yet he shall never prevail against him so as to draw him to the committing of that sin.

From hence we may learn the indulgence of God to weak Christians. While their graces are weak, their temptations shall not be strong. God will not put weak

Christians upon such strong trials as those who have obtained greater measures of grace. Not every man in David's army was put to break through the army of the Philistines, to fetch the waters of the well of Bethlehem, but David's three worthies. God will not put young converts to break through a host of temptations until they shall have obtained experience and strength of grace to grapple with them.

Hence also learn that men of the very strongest and most eminent gifts and graces ought not to presume upon their own strength. "Consider thyself, lest thou also be tempted." You who are most spiritual, take heed lest you be soiled. Some men's pride may make them think they are above ordinances, yet their own experience may satisfy them that they are not above temptations; and certainly, they who are not above temptations will still stand in need of ordinances. Now no man in the world either is or shall be above temptation; if any, surely Adam would yet be in paradise, the best of places, and in innocence, the best of states. But he was not exempted from the temptations of the devil and thereby fell. Therefore let no man presume upon his own strength.

Remember for your comfort that though the devil tempts you with strong temptations, yet he shall never have his will against you. It is true, a godly man may fall into that particular act into which the devil tempts him, yet as to the devil's general aim (the damning of the soul) he shall never have his way. It is a notable expression of our Savior to Peter: "Satan hath desired to sift you as wheat." Satan desired to have him; that was the devil's general aim. Though he may have his will as to a particular act, and you may yield to his temptation, yet he shall never carry you with him into hell.

Remember to your great comfort, you who are the people of God and harassed with the devil's temptations, you who complain that they are great in kind, long in continuance, and the more dangerous because suited to your present condition. Remember that thus the devil dealt with Jesus Christ. His temptations were suited, continued, and of grosser kinds, being to distrust providence, to self-murder, and to blasphemy. And all this was but for your comfort. He suffered being tempted that He might be able to pity you, to have compassion on you, and so succor you, being in the same condition.

Sermon 9

"Be strong in the grace of God, which is in Christ Jesus." 2 Timothy 2:1

CASE 2. We proceed now to a second case of conscience concerning strength of grace. May strength of grace be consistent with strength of lusts and corruptions in the heart?

In answering, I shall speak to these questions:

1. When may corruptions be said to be strong?

2. Why do those who have strong grace have, many times, strong corruptions?

3. What strong corruptions are they most subject to who are strong in grace?

4. In what cases, and with what limitations, may strength of corruptions consist with strength of grace?

QUESTION 1. When may corruptions and lusts be said to be strong in the soul?

1. When sins are committed with complacence. Sin at first is like a snake that is almost starved by reason of the cold and is very weak and feeble, but if it is laid in the bosom then it gathers strength and after awhile sin revives and becomes a delight in the soul. If you were at first troubled at sin, and afterwards take pleasure in sin, it is a sign that sin has a great hand over you. Thus God complained of His people: "What hath My beloved to do in My house? When thou dost evil, then thou rejoicest" (Jeremiah 11:15). We may know the

power and strength of corruption in us by sin's activity in us, and by our cheerfulness and complacency in sin.

2. By the frequency of sin. As a relapse into a disease argues the strength of that infectious humor in the body, so reiterated and multiplied acts of the same sin argue the power and strength of that sin in our hearts. Corruption gathers strength even as grace does, by the frequent acting and exercise of it.

3. When sin is persisted in against the checks of conscience. As it argues the strength of a stream that it bears down before it whatever bank would check the course of it, so it also argues that there is a strong current of corruption in your soul that bears down before it all the warnings, checks, and reproofs of conscience.

QUESTION 2. Why do those who have the strongest graces, many times, also have the strongest corruptions?

1. It arises from the natural temperature and constitution of the body, which disposes men to some sins more than others, although they have such eminence of grace. And hence it is that those who are naturally and constitutionally passionate and given to anger, though they may have a great measure of grace, yet what ado have they to bridle in their anger! What ado to be greatly angry and not greatly sinful! And so such whose temperature inclines them to be lustful, though they have much grace, yet all is little enough to suppress lustful thoughts and wanton looks in them.

2. God suffers this to humble His people and keep them humble under their great measures of grace. It is observable in nature that those creatures that have the most excellence in them have something also of defect

and deformity in them, as if the God of nature did it to keep them humble. The peacock has glittering feathers and yet black feet; the swan has white feathers, but under that a black skin; the eagle has many excellencies—quick sight and high flight—but yet is very ravenous; the camel and elephant are great and stately creatures, but of a deformed shape.

So it is in the state of grace. God suffers some strong and unsubdued corruptions to remain in those who have not only truth, but strength of grace, and this is to keep them humble. Thus Paul, after his great revelations, had a messenger of Satan to buffet him, and a thorn in the flesh to afflict and keep him humble. The thorn in the flesh let the stubborn matter of pride out of his heart. And the consideration of their corruptions much affects the hearts of the godly so that they become more condescending and compassionate to the weak. They depend less upon their own righteousness. They see it is in vain to think of establishing their own righteousness, and that it is too weak a foundation to lay weight and stress of their salvation upon. The covering is too narrow, and the bed is too short for them to rest quietly upon. They are hereby brought to think better of others than themselves, yea, to judge themselves the least of saints, and the greatest of sinners.

3. This is from Satan's malice, who, if he can draw out great corruptions from those who are eminent in grace, he hereby aims to blemish religion and darken the honor of profession. In this case he usually fights against none "great nor small, but the king of Israel," that is, such as are eminent for holiness. When David fell into those great sins of murder and adultery, Satan

had a main end granted him to make the way of true religion stink and be abhorred. Hereby Satan has this end: to embolden those that are weak to sin. The sins and great miscarriages of such as are great professors are great stumbling blocks in the way of the weak to make them fall. Hereby the peace and purity of conscience are violated; the devil will play at small game, rather than at no game, and if he cannot prevail to damn your soul, yet he will endeavor to disquiet your conscience.

QUESTION 3. What strong corruptions are they most subject to who are strong in grace?

1. To lose those strong affections which they first had at their conversion. Holy Greenham complained that it was very difficult to keep together his old discretion and young zeal. Young Christians (as has been already observed) have strong affections, but weak judgments. Their heat is more than their light. Their present apprehension and sense is great and high; their experience is little and low. And so strong Christians who have much grace may find that the flood and flush of affection may be much abated; and it is the fault of old professors that they do not labor to maintain the primitive vigor and vivacity of their first affections. They are too apt to leave their first love; yet we must know they do not decay so as to be bankrupt in grace. In the godly, the decay and declining, though it may be great, yet is neither total nor final. Though he may fail, yet he is not bankrupt; he has still a stock remaining which can never be quite spent, a fountain which can never be quite dry. He has in him "a well of water, springing up to eternal life." The water of a

fountain may be muddied, but it will clear itself again. It may be dammed up in one place, but it will break out in another; so it is with grace.

A tree, you know, in winter season has its fruit and leaves fall off, and it seems as if it were dead; but there is life in the root. So it is in Christians: their beauty and blossom may fall off, their fruit dry up, their leaves drop off, the exercise and the fruits of grace may cease for a time, and yet the root of the matter is in them. It often fares with old professors as it did with old David, of whom it is said that all the clothes he wore could not get or keep heat in him. So it is with Christians: all the duties they perform, and all the ordinances they enjoy, cannot keep up that youthful heart of vigorous affections which once they had.

Many of God's children have not now, as once they had, such complacence in God, such fervency in prayer, such attention in hearing, such delight in Sabbaths, such mournfulness and tenderness of spirit, such a hatred of sin. Now they have not such aggravating thoughts of sin as in former times, nor are the occasions unto sin so avoided as formerly. How many are there who heretofore looked on every sin as a heinous evil, but now do not do so. Time was when every gnat seemed a camel, every mote a beam, and every molehill a mountain; but now they can extenuate and even excuse their sin. Heretofore the most pleasing sin was abominable, the smallest sin detestable, and the lightest sin intolerable; but it is otherwise now through the spiritual decays and abatement in our affections. There are many heretofore who, when they fell into sin, were wont to walk sadly, to sigh deeply, weep bitterly, and pray affectionately; but now they do not these things with those warm and working affections as formerly. The time was when many professors of religion prepared themselves for holy duties with more care, attended to them with more diligence, delighted in them with more complacency, and gained more profit and edification by them than now they do. And that is the first sin, that those who have more grace, both in truth and strength, are apt to fall into spiritual decay.

2. Such as are strong Christians are very subject to spiritual pride, and to be highly conceited of their own gifts, parts, and graces. Spiritual pride is a secret spiritual corruption that is in the most spiritual and gracious heart. It is a bad fruit that grows on the best root. There is nothing better than grace; there is nothing more abominable than sin; there is no sin so bad as pride; there are none so apt to fall into this sin of pride as those who have much grace; there is nothing that weakens a strong Christian more than pride; and nothing argues weakness more than this boasting.

3. To behave themselves with contempt and superciliousness towards weak Christians is an ordinary fault of the strong. There is not any one thing in Scripture more often mentioned than that we should not despise or discourage the weak, which notes an aptness in the strong to be faulty herein. "Let us not judge one another any more." The word notes they were wont to do so before. Spiritual pride is a root of bitterness, which bears these two bitter fruits: an overvaluing of ourselves and an undervaluing of other men's persons and gifts.

4. Strong Christians are apt to put too much duty and talk upon the weak. John's disciples failed towards the disciples of Christ about fasting. Strong Christians should deal tenderly with the weak; they should excuse

their failings, conceal their weaknesses, commend their performances, cherish their forwardness, resolve their doubts, bear their burdens, and hereby make the way of religion to be lovely and amiable to them, whereas by their severe austerity the weak are disheartened at their first entrance.

5. The strong may not be content with measures of grace. How apt are those who have grace to say in one sense, as the rich man said in another, "Soul, take thine ease, thou hast goods laid up for many years" (Luke 12:19). And hereupon many grow slack and careless in holy duties, and do not improve ordinances for the increase of their graces. The best of Christians are apt to fall into satiety, than which nothing can be more prejudicial to the soul. The devil tempts those who have but a little grace to think they have none, and those who have more grace to think they have enough. The best are apt to mistake themselves in thinking that there is a just dimension and full growth of grace attainable in this life. Whereas, indeed, the best improvement of having much grace is to desire more, and not to be satisfied with any measure of grace "till we come to a perfect man, unto the measure of the stature of the fullness of Christ" (Ephesians 4:13). And that is not attainable in this life.

Perfection is the aim of this life, but it is the reward of another life. We should endeavor after perfection in grace, but we shall not attain it till grace is perfected in glory.

QUESTION 4. In what cases, and with what limitations, may strength of corruptions consist with strength of grace?

ANSWER. The resolving of this question is of very much use to the soul; for the soul that is overmastered with strong corruptions may not only question the strength of his grace, but the being of it. How may I then know that I have both the truth and strength of grace in me, though I am overpowered sometimes by strong and prevailing corruptions? You may know by these things:

1. If you maintain in you a strong opposition against your corruptions. We know that the flesh lusts against the spirit, but does the spirit lust against the flesh? Though you cannot fully subdue sin, yet do you strongly oppose it? If so, there is grace and strength of sin; but an irreconcilable opposition to sin argues the strength of grace. Strength of grace is not so much seen in those particular acts of suppression and actual overcoming of it as in that constant and habitual frame of heart in opposing sin.

2. Though sin is strong, yet grace may be strong too in your soul. If you have a strong measure of humiliation, though sin is great, if your sorrow is great too, it evidences your grace is so also. It was a great grace in Manasseh that he humbled himself greatly, though he had been a very great sinner.

3. If you have strong cries to God against your sins, this argues grace, though it is ready to be deflowered by your corruptions. If, when corruptions and temptations prevail, you pray to the Lord with strong cries and tears, this argues grace, yea, and the strength of grace.

4. If you have strong affections that carry you to Christ, certainly you have grace, though your strong corruptions often carry you from Christ. Peter had

more infirmities, corruptions, and sins than all the disciples besides (except Judas). He took Christ aside, gave Him carnal counsel, and said as to His sufferings: "Far be it from Thee, Lord, this shall not be unto Thee," for which Christ said to him, "Get thee behind Me, Satan." He dreams of merit, and boasts of what he had done for Christ: "Behold, we have forsaken all and followed Thee; what shall we have therefore?" Peter, of all the disciples, was the most confident of his own strength, and boasted of what he would do and suffer for Christ: "Though all men should be offended because of Thee, yet will I never be offended. And if I should die with Thee, yet will I not deny Thee."

Nay, and presently after this confident undertaking, Peter denied Christ, and swore and cursed that he knew Him not. Some observe that Peter's cursing was not only his cursing of himself if he knew Christ, but that he also cursed Jesus Christ so that he might appear to them to be not one of His disciples.

And yet, notwithstanding all this, Peter had not only truth and reality, but eminence and strength of grace, for though temptations and corruptions sometimes prevailed, yet he had strong affections towards Jesus Christ. He did and suffered that which few or none of the disciples did. He was the man who, of all the disciples, wept most bitterly for his sins. Peter was the first who ran to the sepulcher, and went into the sepulcher to see what had become of Christ. He was the man who, hearing that Christ was risen and on the seashore, leapt into the sea for joy. He was the man who made the first sermon and first preached the gospel after the ascension of Christ. He had that love for Christ which was as strong as death, for he suffered death and was crucified (as ecclesiastical writers say), but would not be crucified but with his heels up, deeming it too great an honor to be crucified in the same manner that his Lord and Master was. So the strength of his affections argued, notwithstanding his great failings, the strength of grace in him.

Now I will make some application of what has been spoken in this case of conscience.

Though, in the case before mentioned, strength of grace may be consistent with strength of corruptions, yet there are other cases wherein they are altogether inconsistent. Those are:

1. When the strength and workings of corruptions are not clearly discovered to the soul, for grace always, as a light set up in the soul, discovers the darkness of corruption.

2. Where corruptions are not sensibly bewailed, it is to be feared that there is not strength of grace.

3. Where occasions for those strong, prevailing sins and corruptions are not heedfully avoided. Certainly, if you have grace to make you sensible of what corruptions you are vulnerable to, your grace will make you walk so circumspectly as to avoid all occasions leading thereto.

4. If they are not strongly resisted, and the beginning of each corruption not diligently suppressed, in this case, strength of grace and strength of corruption, are utterly inconsistent.

5. Though there may be strong grace and strong corruption in the soul, yet the reign of any one corruption is utterly inconsistent with grace and the strength of it. "Let not sin reign in your mortal bodies. Sin shall

not have dominion over you, for you are not under the law, but under grace" (Romans 6:12, 14)—which is not to be understood in the antinomian sense, that believers are not under the mandatory power of the moral law, but the meaning of the word "law," as Beza interprets it, is the law of sin. And so the Apostle Paul in Romans 7:23 means a law in his members that warred against the law of his mind, and brought him into captivity to the law of sin; that is, sin had sway in him with the power and force of a law. And this argued the strength of grace in Paul, that though he was overborne by the strength of sin and corruption, and taken prisoner by it, yet he never yielded to it as to a lawful sovereign. For so he added in verse 25: "So then with the mind I serve the law of God, but with my flesh the law of sin." It may be said of the corruptions in God's children what was shown to Daniel concerning the beasts: "they had their dominion taken away, yet their lives were prolonged for a season" (Daniel 7:12).

6. When we see there is a consistency between grace and corruption. I would have spiritual and inward corruptions understood as meaning hardness of heart, spiritual pride, and deadness in duties, for into gross, external, open acts of evil strong Christians seldom fall.

7. We must also be further informed that if we consider particular acts of sin, some one lust may seem to be more strong in a godly Christian than in a mere mortal man. For instance, in the case of lust, when we consider how David abused his neighbor's wife, and how Abimelech would not touch another's wife, one would have judged David the heathen and Abimelech the believer; and therefore the strength of grace or

corruption must not be judged by any one particular place where some impetuous temptation has prevailed.

8. Last, we are to know that a corruption may be really weakened when sensibly strong. As a man in a fever is seemingly strong, but is really weak, so corruption may be then most enfeebled when in our apprehension it is most enraged. It may rave and rage most when it is being crucified. As a coal glows most just before it is going out, and a candle burned down in the socket gives a blaze a little before it is extinct, so it is when corruption is ready to expire.

In a mere mortal man, sin may be restrained when it is not subdued; corruption may be quiet where it is not mortified, where it yet may rage as if unrestrained. A man's last gasp may be the strongest breath. So when corruption is ready to give up the ghost, it may seem to breathe strongest. As a bird may flutter when its neck is broken, so sin may seemingly resist grace when the power, strength, and life of it is utterly broken.

Sermon 10

"Be strong in the grace of God, which is in Christ Jesus." 2 Timothy 2:1

We have already handled two great cases of conscience, about strength of grace and about the consistency of strong temptations and strong corruptions with the strength of grace, and shall now proceed to a third case:

CASE 3. May strength of grace consist with the want of those strong affections which Christians have had at their first conversion?

In answering I shall endeavor to show three things:

When a man may be said to lose his first affections.

In what cases a strong Christian may want strong affections.

Whence it is that those who have strong grace may want such strong affections as they had at their first conversion.

When may a Christian be said to lose his first affections?

Affections are fitly compared to the pulses of the soul by which judgment may be given of the state and temper of the soul. And that we may know when these affections beat low and are decayed, we may make judgment hereof:

1. When we have not such eager desires after duties. It is very remarkable that at a Christian's first con-

version, he is so eager and earnest after holy duties that he will hardly allow time for the duties of his particular calling; nay, how have men at first tied themselves to hear so many sermons, make so many prayers, read so many chapters, spend so many hours in holy meditation by themselves and in good conference with other Christians! But alas, afterwards this fervor begins to cool and remit, and men pray less, and hear more seldom, and this is from the multitude of their worldy occasions. Usually men at their conversion, which, as divines have observed, ordinarily falls out between the eighteenth and twenty-eighth year of their age (though God, indeed, is tied to no year), yet at that age usually have less of the world; and so it comes to pass that afterwards, when the cares and profits and pleasures of the world steal away their affections, they grow much more remiss than they were at the beginning.

2. Affections may be judged to be decayed when men have not such ravishing joys as they were wont to have. How many have been at first in David's frame of heart: "I was glad when they said to me, 'Let us go into the house of the Lord' " (Psalm 122:1)! But afterwards the overflowing of this flood of joy by degrees has abated.

3. When sensible profit by ordinance is abated. A man may profit by ordinances, and yet not be sensible of his profiting. A Christian may grow at the root in solidity of grace, though he may not shoot up so much in blossoms of affection.

In what cases may a strong Christian want strong affections?

1. You may have less sin in duties, though less affections. Weak, young converts have oftentimes much
affection in holy duties, but much corruption too.
They are very subject to rashness and precipitance in
their prayers, to be proud of any small measure of
grace in duty, and too apt to have carnal dependence
upon their duties. But old, experienced Christians, as
they have often less affection, so less sin in duties.
Papists have very much affection in the performance of
their devotions, but, alas, they have the leaven of this
error in the best duties: they think they earn merit by
them. But grown and knowing Christians, though they
may not be so affectionate in duty as the weak, yet may
exercise much more grace than they do.

And so also it is after duties are performed. Weak
Christians are apt to indulge their corruptions afterwards, thinking they have made a compensation for
their sins by their duties; but an experienced, grown
Christian, though not so affectionate in duty, yet is
careful afterwards that he does not by sin spoil all his
duties.

2. A strong Christian may want strong affections if
he has strength of judgment to recompense the want
of his affections. Young trees are more sappy, but old
trees are more solid; wherefore the Apostle prays for
the Philippians, not only that their love might abound,
but that their judgment might also abound. A man
who has come to his full age, though he does not grow
in bulk and extension of parts, yet he grows intensively,
and in the consolidation of the parts of his body. Old
and experienced Christians, though they have not so
much affection, yet have more solidity and clearness of
judgment, more experimental knowledge in the pro-

found mysteries of the gospel, and more distinct apprehensions of the deep things of Christ. What a strong believer wants in affections, he has compensated to him in a distinct and experimental knowledge of the deceitfulness of his heart, of the vanity of the world, of the sinfulness of sin, and of the transcendent excellence of Christ. New converts are rash, inconsiderate, and injudicious; and therefore we have a promise made to new converts that they should *proceed* in grace.

It is a promise made to the Gentiles, when the kingdom of Christ shall come among them, that though at first they were rash, yet it is said, "The heart of the rash shall understand knowledge, and the tongue of the stammerers shall be ready to speak plainly" (Isaiah 32:4). Affection without knowledge will be but rashness, which (like mettle in a young horse) will be apt to make him hurry and stumble. An experienced Christian, though he has not so much seeming mettle in his affections, yet shall ride more on the way to heaven by far than a young convert, and that without fear of stumbling. At the first kindling of the fire, there may be more smoke, though afterward the flame will be clearer. So when at first you have much affection, afterwards you shall have a clearer judgment.

3. A strong Christian may want strong affections in accordance with his natural temper, and not from a careless distemper. There are some persons who are naturally of a soft and tender disposition, and these are naturally more affectionate. Nay, the woman, who is the weaker vessel, commonly in her heart holds more affection. And so, likewise, there are some who naturally are more bound up in their affections, and

are of the reserved temper, who naturally do not break out into any great expression, either of the passion of joy or grief.

We read in the gospel that those who expressed the most affection to Christ at His death, and made the most passionate lamentation for Him, were the women, who naturally are of a more melting disposition. Some men's dispositions are like ice: they will easily thaw and melt; others are like iron, and it must be a hot fire that will melt them down. So it is that some men will be more affectionate upon a small occasion than others upon a greater, and this is from natural disposition. Melanchthon was not as affectionate as Luther, but it is observed that he was more judicious.

4. In case of sickness and old age, and bodily weakness, he who has strength of grace may yet want strength of affection. The expression of our affection depends much upon the temperature of the body; if bodily strength and vigor are impaired, our affections must flag. As the ebbing and flowing of the sea depend upon the motion and influence of the moon, so our affections ebb and flow according as the strength or weakness of the body has an influence on them. As a musician, when he is grown old, cannot so dexterously handle an instrument as when he was young (though perhaps he has now more judgment and experience in music), so old age brings experience in the ways of God, yet may abate affections. Old age and sickness make the body like a tired horse to the active soul; an active traveller would fain ride away to his journey's end, but his horse is tired. An aged, sickly Christian may have as much grace and more than he had at first, and yet not be so able to pray. A minister may not be

so able to preach affectionately as before, due to the indispositions of the body.

Whence is it that those that have strength of grace, may yet want those affections which they had at their first conversion?

1. Because at first conversion grace was but particularly employed. When much water runs in one channel, it makes the stream stronger; but when there are many rivulets cut out, though there is as much and more water, yet there's not the same strength of stream. So it is at our first conversion: all our affections make up but one stream, and so our affections seem the stronger. A new convert has not so many duties to perform as a grown Christian has, because he does not know so many duties. It may be at first that all his affections run out to pray, hear the Word, and read good books; and while all the affections run in this one channel they seem to be very strong. Whereas a grown Christian has not only these general duties, but many particular duties of his calling and relations to follow. He has many duties to perform to God and men which a new convert knows not; and therefore it is that, though his affections may seem weaker, yet his grace is as strong as before, and stronger.

2. This is from the newness of the condition. Naturally we are much affected with any new things. For example, if a man who has been many years in a dark dungeon is suddenly brought into the light, the suddenness of the change would much affect that man. This is the state of our souls at our first conversion; we are thereby "brought from darkness into light, and from the power of Satan unto God" (Acts 26:18). By

the grace of conversion, God calls us "out of darkness into His marvelous light" (1 Peter 2:9). And because it is so marvelous, therefore it so much affects. The change at first conversion is very great; a man becomes another man, and is also so affected that he is put into a kind of astonishment. Yet in this case we must distinguish between solid affections and floating, transient passions which wear off presently and vanish suddenly.

The affections of some Christians, especially young ones, are like those colors which are not in grain; they will soon fade. It is with a young convert as with a man going to execution: when he is upon the ladder, and a pardon is unexpectedly brought, how will this man be transported with joy! He will leap for joy; he will in that case be all joy and exultation for his present, and it may be that afterward the flush and torrent of his joy is abated, though his life is as dear to him as ever.

So when the soul has been brought by the law of God to a sight of its lost condition, and then the gospel has proclaimed a pardon, and the Spirit of God has set the comfort of that pardon upon his heart, oh, what ravishments has that soul for the present which perhaps he shall not long retain! The violence of his joy is abated, but the solidity of it remains. The soul is much affected with its first meeting with Christ, and though the flush of that joy is over, yet the soul's love for Christ is as much, and its prized communion with Christ the same. When the cripple was restored to strength, he went leaping and praising God because the unexpectedness of the cure mightily affected his heart.

And this is a second reason why those who are

grown and solid Christians, perhaps, may not retain the same measure of affections they had at their first conversion.

3. A third reason may be taken from God's indulgence to a young convert, which He usually gives in comfort according to the necessity of His people. It is with God our heavenly Father as with our natural parents: they are most tender over their newborn children. The parable of the returning prodigal is very full to this purpose: his father not only received him mercifully, but bountifully too; he gave him more than was for necessity; not only shoes, but a ring; not only clothes, but the best robe; not only bread, but the fatted calf; and music at this feast also. And all this was for this newly converted and repenting son, though his father did not entertain him so every day. So our God, at our first conversion, expresses much of His bounty and indulgence to His children, though afterward we may have the same love of God, and the same love for God, though the expressions may not be the same now, as formerly in those days of God's bounty.

Let us learn from hence that, though we have lost those affections which we had, yet we must labor to be sensible of, and humbled for, those decays. A decayed condition is an uncomfortable condition. Though you have so much grace as will bring you to heaven, yet by your decays you will be uncomfortable here upon earth. We must labor to get those decays repaired. If you have left your first love, "repent and do thy first works" (Revelation 2:5). We must make up the want of former affections in solidity of knowledge and judgment; and if the candle gives not so great a blaze, let it give a more clear and constant light. We must labor to keep up the primitive vigor of our affections.

Remember you may lose that in a short time which you may be a long time in recovering. A man may lose more strength in one week's sickness than many months will make reparation. A wound may be quickly made, but not so soon cured. Philosophers will tell us that the way from the habit to the privation is far easier than from the privation to the habit; it is far easier to make a seeing man blind than to make a blind man see. So it is far easier to lose our holy affections than it is to recover them.

Labor to keep up your holy affections, for the truth of grace is more discerned by our affections than by our actions. Acts of grace may be easier dissembled than gracious affections. A painter may paint the color, but not the heart of the fire.

Labor to keep up affections as they were at first, because it is very hard to retain them. It is hard to keep them wound up to any height. Flush of spiritual joys is like the sea: the tide does not so flow, but the ebb does fall as low. Bernard said of these strong gusts, and the great flush of these spiritual joys and gracious affections, "They come but suddenly, and stay but a short time." As in nature there's a spring and then the fall of the leaf, and one day is clear and another is cloudy, so it is with the best Christian: his affections are not always at the same pitch or at the same height; but it should be our endeavor to cherish and maintain in our souls our first flourishing affections, in and toward the ways of God.

Sermon 11

"Be strong in the grace of God, which is in Christ Jesus." 2 Timothy 2:1

CASE 4. Having dispatched three cases of conscience concerning strength of grace, I now proceed to a fourth: May a man who has strength of grace want the comfort of his grace?

ANSWER. I shall answer this question affirmatively. A man who has the strength of grace may yet want the comfort of it. Strength of grace (as you have heard) does not exempt a man from temptations of the devil, nor from desertions from God. It is an undoubted rule: there may be strength of grace where there is not the comfort and evidence of it. A child of light may walk in darkness for a time; and though he has the Holy Ghost working and increasing grace in his heart, yet he may want the oil of gladness, though he has received a precious anointing of grace. A child of God, as to his spiritual condition, may for a time be in the same condition that Paul and the mariners were in, "who for many days had neither sun nor stars appearing, being under no small tempest, hopes of being saved being taken away." So it fares with God's dearest children: they may be in the dark, and can see no light; they may have the graces of the Spirit, and yet want the comforts of the Spirit.

In the opening of this point, I shall proceed.

I will thus prove from Scripture that a child of God

may be strong in grace, and yet want the comfort of his grace. I will lay down reasons why it is thus. I will lay down some directions how those who have grace, and yet want the comfort of their graces, should procure unto themselves the comfort of their graces. And then I shall commend some comfortable considerations to such as have grace, but want the comfort of it.

First, I shall give you instances, both in the Old and New Testament, that those who have been strong in grace have wanted comfort.

Job was a man eminent for grace, "a perfect and upright man, and one that feared God, and eschewed evil," and yet Job complained: "Wherefore hidest Thou Thy face, and holdest me for Thine enemy?" Nay, God not only hid His face, but handled him as His enemy; for thus he made his moan: "He teareth me in His wrath." That refers to God, not to the devil, nor to Job's unmerciful enemies or uncharitable friends. "He teareth me (that is, God teareth me), who in my apprehension hateth me, and gnasheth upon me with His teeth, and as an enemy sharpeneth His eyes upon me." These sad apprehensions were upon Job that God was his enemy; see him further lamenting: "He hath destroyed me on every side, and I am gone, and my hope hath He removed as a tree; He hath also kindled His wrath against me, and counteth me unto Him as one of His enemies." Yea, destruction from God was a terror to him.

Asaph, a holy man, yet complained: "Will the Lord cast off forever, and will He be favorable no more? Is His mercy clean gone forever? Doth His promise fail for evermore? Hath God forgotten to be gracious? Hath He in anger shut up His tender mercies?" (Psalm

77:7–9). These are the sad expostulations of a troubled spirit, cast down under deep dejection, and in the dark by reason of the suspension of divine favor.

David was "a man after God's own heart," whose gracious breathings through the whole book of Psalms show that he was a man of an excellent spirit, and had much grace; yet David wanted the comfort of his grace when his soul was cast down, and his spirit was disquieted within him.

Heman was a man so eminent for wisdom that the Holy Ghost used him as an instance of wisdom: "as wise as Heman." And yet in the 88th Psalm was a strain of as sad a complaint as you shall meet with in the whole book of God: "Thou hast laid me in the lowest pit, in darkness, in the deep: Thy wrath lieth hard upon me, and Thou hast afflicted me with Thy waves" (88:6–7). So little comfort had these holy men, though they were eminent in grace.

It is true of many dear children of God what is said of the apostles and disciples of Christ: "Whither I go (said Christ), ye know, and the way ye know" (John 14:4). To which speech of Christ Thomas answered in the next verse: "Lord, we know not whither Thou goest, and how can we know the way?" Augustine thus reconciled this: they knew where Christ went, but they dared not once believe that they had such knowledge; they did not know their own knowledge. The expressions of Christ were different from those words of Thomas. The Lord Jesus spoke as it was, and Thomas spoke as he thought. The apostle had grace, and yet wanted the comfort and assurance of it. I will not speak here of the Lord Jesus, who, though He was full of grace and truth, yet wanted comfort when He was in that bitter agony and cried out: "My God, My God, why hast Thou forsaken Me!" Indeed, in the New Testament there are not so many instances of those who wanted the comfort of their graces as we find in the Old Testament. And the reason is this: profession, at the first publishing and promulgation of the gospel, met with so many sharp afflictions that God indulged them, and made their inward consolations to abound as their outward sufferings did abound. However, the previously mentioned instances may suffice to prove that it is true that believers who are strong in grace may yet want the comfort of their graces.

To give you some grounds of this, the reason may be drawn either from God, from ourselves, or from the devil.

The first reason is from the Lord. He withholds from them to whom He has given grace the comfort of their graces:

1. To manifest His divine authority and absolute sovereignty over His people. As the natural light of the day and the darkness of the night are at God's disposal, so also are the spiritual light of comfort and the darkness of the deserted and dejected spirit. God gives divine and spiritual consolations, out of the goodness of His will, and withdraws Himself to show the absoluteness and sovereign liberty of His will.

2. To let His people know that comfort is not effectual to holiness, neither inseparably nor necessarily belonging to grace—though there cannot be true grace where there is no peace.

3. To show that God, in the dispensations both of grace and comfort, shows Himself a free and gracious agent; and all our graces which God works in us are

merely from God's grace to us. He will give comfort when and to whom He wills, but still, as a reward of His own free grace, the comfort of a pardon. The comfortable knowledge of our pardon is as much from God's free grace as the pardon itself; and therefore God suspends the comforts of grace to make us look up to Him for it. When you repent, God gives a pardon; but therein He rewards His own work in you. To give a pardon, or a sense of pardon, is an act of mere liberality in God.

4. To put a difference between heaven and earth. Heaven is a place for comfort, earth for duty; earth is for the getting of grace, heaven for the rewarding of grace. Our Lord Jesus Christ, like the good master of the feast, reserves the best for the last. The sons of nobles, when they travel into foreign parts, have no more allowance than what will accommodate their travels; the inheritance is reserved for them when they come to their father's house. So believers who are strangers and pilgrims here have so much grace and comfort as befits their passage to heaven; but they have an inheritance, incorruptible and undefiled, that fades not away, but is reserved in the heavens. God thinks it not fit to give constant comforts in an inconstant world; nor full comforts in an empty world; nor lasting comforts in a transitory world.

The second reason may be taken from ourselves, and that in many regards. Those who have much grace yet may have but a little comfort; and this may spring from a threefold root in us: from something that is merely natural in us, from something that is spiritual and good, or from something that is evil in us.

This may arise from the prevalence of a natural

melancholy in the body, whereby the understanding may be darkened, the fancy troubled, reason perverted, and the soul saddened. Melancholy is the mother of discomfort and the nurse of doubting. It was (as some think) depth of melancholy that prevailed upon Nebuchadnezzar, so that he did not know, while under the power of that distemper, whether he was a man or a beast. And in the like manner this bodily melancholy may so far distemper your soul that you who have grace yet may not know whether you are a child of God or a child of the devil. It is no more wonder to see a melancholy man doubt and question his spiritual condition than it is to see a child cry when beaten or to hear a sick man groan.

You may silence a melancholy man when you are not able to comfort him; and though you may resolve his doubts and scruples by evident and convincing answers and arguments, yet let such a man retire alone and brood over his melancholy thoughts, and by the prevalence of this perturbing humor all is forgotten, and he is as unsatisfied as if you had said nothing to him. And you may perceive that it is the power of melancholy that is the cause of a man's distemper when he is very much troubled and yet can give no distinct account of any particular thing that troubles him.

This discomfort often arises from that which is good in us, from that holy jealousy and tenderness of conscience which makes a child of God suspect and inquire into his condition. And though he has true grace, yet he is afraid lest all be but a delusion. In such cases, the soul so pores over sin and infirmities that it cannot see its own evidences. A tender conscience is more apt to be dejected by the sight of sin than to be comforted in the sense of grace; and the reason for this is because sin more directly falls under the cognizance of our conscience, especially a natural conscience. "The works of the flesh are manifest" (Galatians 5:19), but the fruits of grace and of the Spirit are not so easily discerned.

This discomfort, usually from a root of bitterness, appears even in the best of God's children, and is that whereby God punishes the sins of His people for:

1. Their quenching the motions of the Spirit. If you grieve the Spirit of God, it is just with God to grieve your spirits. You never send God's Spirit sad to heaven but God may make sad your spirits on earth.

2. Slightiness and fearlessness of heart towards God. When children grow saucy, peremptory, and froward before their parents, it is no wonder if a father's frown corrects that irreverence. Most of those who lie uncomfortably under a sense of the displeasure of God may rest themselves too much upon His love, and grow secure and fearless to offend God. God loves to have His children come near Him in a holy confidence that He is their Father, but yet to keep their distance by humble reverence.

3. Another sin that God punishes in His children, by withholding comfort from those who are in grace, is their superciliousness, contempt, and lack of compassion towards others who are but weak in grace. God's own people are very much to blame herein for rigor and unmercifulness towards those who are weak in the faith, despising all who are inferior to them in gifts and graces, whereby they often "break the bruised reed and quench the smoking flax" (Matthew 12:20), and lack bowels of pity and tenderness towards their brethren.

*IT IS THE SPIRIT OF GOD THAT GRIEVES WITHIN US THAT WE FEEL

To take down pride, God often brings such, even His own people, to be low in comfort. And it is just that they should want comfort who have neglected to comfort and cherish those who were weak in grace.

4. Growing cold, lazy, and heedless in holy duties. If we put off God without true service, God may justly put us off without true comfort. This rule holds in spiritual affairs: he who will not work shall not eat. If we abate in the sanctifying work of the Spirit, it is but just that God withholds the comforting work of the Spirit. "The sluggard," said Solomon, "hath poverty enough." So if we grow lazy and sluggish in holy duties, it is just that our stock of comfort decay. Though holy duties do not merit comforts, yet comfort usually rises and falls according to our diligence in duties. True grace is never so apparent to, and sensible in, the soul as when it is in action; and therefore want of exercise must cause want of comfort. As fire in the flint is never seen or felt till it is struck out by the steel, so is grace, and the comfort of grace is never so sensible as when it is exercised much in holy duties.

OUR LOSS OF AWARDS & BLESSING NOT WITHHOLDING BY GOD

5. Any one sin indulged by or concealed in the conscience is enough to mar all your comfort. Concealed guilt contracts horror. The candle will never burn clearly while there is an abnormality in it.

Sin in the conscience is like a Jonah in the ship who caused a tempest. The conscience is like a troubled sea whose waters cannot rest; it is like a mote in the eye which causes a perpetual trouble while it is there; it is like the wind gathered in the caverns of the earth, which makes earthquakes and terrible eruptions. It is just with God that a man's own iniquities should correct him, and his backsliding should reprove him.

Concealed guilt, though it may not bring a child of God to hell, yet for a time may bring hell into his conscience. So by all these particulars we may see that if our comforts are abated, we may thank ourselves for it.

The third reason is taken from the restless malice of Satan who, when he cannot do the greater, will do the less; if he cannot damn your soul, he will labor all he can to disquiet your conscience. The devil aims principally to make us walk sinfully, and if not so then uncomfortably; if he cannot make us live without God and Christ and grace in the world, then he endeavors to make us live outside the comfort of our grace. And hence it is that many dear children of God have truth and strength of grace in them, yet hearkening too much to Satan, live outside the comfort of their grace.

QUESTION 3. But what shall I do, who want the comfort of my grace, to procure it that I may have comfort answerable to grace?

1. Live more in the exercise of grace; and that is the ready way not only to increase grace, but to obtain the comfort of grace. It was the apostolic salutation: "Grace and peace be multiplied." If grace is multiplied (and it will be by the exercise of it), then peace will also be multiplied. The work of righteousness shall be peace; and the effect of righteousness shall be quietness and assurance forever. "Great peace have they which love Thy law, and nothing shall offend them" (Psalm 119:165).

2. Leave no sin unrepented of; take heed of guilt of sin lying on the conscience; take away the abnormality from the candle and it will burn clearly. "If iniquity be

in thy hand, put it far from thee, and let not wickedness dwell in thy tabernacles; for thou shalt then lift up thy face without spot; yea, thou shalt be steadfast, <u>and shalt not fear</u>" (Job 11:14–15). "Behold now," answered Job, "I have ordered my cause, I know that I shall be justified" (Job 13:18). The more ordered our ways are, the more steady and full are our comforts; the more sin in the soul, the less comfort in that soul.

3. Call to mind former experiences that your soul has had of God. Thus did David when, by reason of the discomfort of his soul, he cried out, "Why art thou cast down, O my soul, and why art thou disquieted in me? O my God, my soul is cast down within me; therefore will I remember Thee from the land of Jordan, and of the Hermonites" (Psalm 42:5–6). In other words, "I will remember Thee, and what Thou didst at Jordan, when Thou didst dry up the river, and Thy people passed on dry land into Canaan." "And I will remember the land of Hermonites," that is, what He did unto Og, king of Bashan, and to Sihon king of the Amorites, for Hermon was part of the country of those kings. So the Psalmist was under great discomfort when he cried, "Will the Lord cast off forever? Is His mercy clean gone from me?" (Psalm 77:7). But he recovered himself out of that sad case by remembering former experiences, for so he added in verses 11–12: "I will remember the works of the Lord; surely I will remember Thy wonders of old. I will meditate on all Thy works, and talk of Thy doings." Past experiences should be present encouragements.

4. Attribute to God the glory of His own grace; this is the way to enjoy the comfort of our grace. Say with the church, "Not unto us, not unto us, O Lord, but

unto Thy name give the glory." It will be just with God to deny you the comfort of grace if you deny Him the glory of His grace. Want of comfort is God's medicine to cure our souls of spiritual pride; and humble thankfulness for the least grace is the way to enjoy the comfort of all our graces.

5. Spend more time in cherishing your comforts than in questioning them. It is the fault of some Christians to spend more time in fruitless complaints of the want of comfort than in faithful endeavors after comfort in God's way. There are those who are more inquisitive how they lost their comforts than they are careful how to recover them; and so indeed they weaken their own hands, but strengthen the hands of Satan.

Finally, what may be the comfortable considerations which may be gathered from the truth delivered, that strong Christians may be but weak in comfort?

Now the handling of this last will be an application of the other three particulars, by way of consolation to those who may perhaps now have strong grace but weak comfort.

1. The godly are never without the ground of comfort, though they may be without the sense of comfort. Though they may be without present feeling, yet they do not want real cause of consolation. They have an undoubted right to comfort, though not a clear sight of comfort. A child may have right to an inheritance, though he is not able to demonstrate and prove his right. Perhaps a man cannot read his evidences for his land, and yet those evidences give him a right to his land. So it is with a child of God: he has comfort sown,

though perhaps he cannot presently reap it. "Light is sown for the righteous, and joy for the upright heart." It was so with Hagar in the wilderness of Beersheba; her water was spent in the bottle, and she cast her child away from her because she could not endure to see him die. She lifted up her voice and wept that she and her child should both miserably perish by thirst, and yet there was a well of water near by her, but she saw it not. So it is with many a poor soul who is thirsty for comfort and (as they think) ready to perish, and yet there is a well of water of life and comfort near by, but they want the eye of faith to see it. And this is a great comfort that a child of God has: though he may want comfort, yet he has a right to comfort in that he has truth of grace.

2. At that time when God withholds comfort from you, yet He really loves you. Jesus Christ sometimes serves His children as Joseph served his brethren. He spoke roughly to them and put them in prison, yet Joseph dearly loved his brethren; his bowels yearned towards them. Thus Jesus Christ's real love is the same toward His children at all times, though the manifestation of it may not be always alike. Joseph knew his brethren, though his brethren did not know him. "The Lord knows who are His," though those who are His, perhaps, do not know that they are so. Jesus knew Mary, though she did not know Him.

3. There may be much mercy to us in withdrawing of comfort. There may be as much goodness of God manifested in the withdrawing of comfort as in the giving of comfort. God many times in wrath lets a man be filled with the ungrounded comfort of supposed grace. O beloved, it is far better to want comfort than grace!

Many a man who has no true grace, yet has seeming comfort; but a child of God is often without comfort so that he may examine and exercise his grace, and so at last enjoy a well-grounded joy and a well-bottomed consolation. Grace is the best foundation of spiritual consolation.

Sermon 12

"Be strong in the grace of God, which is in Christ Jesus." 2 Timothy 2:1

I have already handled four cases of conscience concerning strength of grace:

1. Whether strong temptations may be consistent with strength of grace.

2. Whether strong corruptions may consist with strength of grace.

3. Whether a man may be strong in grace, and yet want those strong affections which he had at his first conversion.

4. Whether a man may have strength of grace and yet want the comfort of his grace.

CASE 5. I shall now proceed to a fifth case of conscience: May a man be said to have strength of grace who has but weak gifts?

In the opening of this case, I shall thus proceed:

1. I will premise some positions.

2. I shall positively resolve the case.

3. And then I will give you some practical inferences, by way of application.

I will begin with the first, namely, the premises, and there are five:

The first premise is this: though all believers have the same Spirit, yet God in His wisdom thinks it fit that they shall not have the same gifts. "There are diversities of gifts, but the same Spirit" (1 Corinthians 12:4). It is so with flowers: there is not the same smell, but different smells to different flowers, and yet all their scents have the same influences from above. It is just so with instruments of music: there are divers sounds in the organ, but the same breath causes the several sounds. So, in the church of God, though there are the same influences of the Spirit of God, yet there is not the same measure of gifts in each member of the church.

The second premise is this: diversity of gifts is not to be ascribed to man's industry, diligence, or education, but to the free pleasure and dispensation of God. It is true, much may be ascribed to study, industry, and diligence in terms of developing one's gifts, which was the ground of the Apostle's exhortation: "give attendance to reading, to exhortation, to doctrine, and meditate on these things; give thyself wholly to them, that thy profiting may appear to all" (1 Timothy 4:13, 15). The Apostle speaks there of profiting in ministerial gifts, which gifts diligence and study much develop and promote. Yet though we were all equal in study and diligence, there would be a diversity in our gifts, lest men should boast of their industry in acquiring gifts and thereby exclude God's bounty in bestowing them. Psalm 127:1: "Except the Lord build the house, they labor in vain that build it." Arthur Hildersham wrote: "Suppose that two men were to read the same books, and to study the same matter every day, yet the one may be a dunce, and a man of low gifts, and the other may have rare parts, and excellent endowments; this is to show who we are beholden to, that is, God, whose dispensations of gifts are many, and variously bestowed." Hence it is that the Apostle told us that "all these gifts worketh that one and the self-same Spirit, dividing to every man severally as He wills" (1 Corinthians 12:11). So though one man differs from another in gifts, yet it is God who makes him to differ.

The third premise is this: a man may be excellent in one gift and yet defective in other gifts; one man shall not have all. This is very observable by instances in Scripture. The first instance is between Paul and Barnabas. If you look unto Paul, his gift was the gift of utterance and freedom of speech, inasmuch that at Lystra Paul was taken for Mercury, the god of eloquence, because he was the chief speaker. And though it is said of Paul that "he was rude of speech," that is not as if it were so indeed, but in the opinion and conceit of the Corinthians, who, being seduced by false teachers, hearkened to their disparagements of Paul.

Paul was a most eloquent man, and had much of the gift of utterance; but now Barnabas exceeded Paul in another gift: comforting those who were troubled in conscience. He was a "son of consolation," to comfort troubled consciences. So it is likewise in the case of Peter and the other apostles. Divines gather this from Christ's commission to Peter, singling him out when He said, "Peter, feed my lambs; Peter, lovest thou Me?" The reason some expositors give why Peter was singled out was that Peter had an excellent gift in preaching and in feeding the lambs of Christ, that is, weak believers. Moreover, it is said of James and John that they were called "sons of thunder," as having a more powerful gift from God to terrify and awaken a sinner's conscience than Peter and the other apostles had. So though some of the apostles had most excellent gifts, yet some of them exceeded others in some particular gift.

The fourth premise is this: there are cases wherein men may have great gifts, but weak grace. God is pleased sometimes to carry men's gifts very high when their graces have not a proportionate elevation. And the reason is that gifts are for the good of others, for the edification of the church of God, and not for the good of a man's self only. The Corinthians were wanting in no gift and had all knowledge; and yet when he mentioned their graces he said, "I could not speak to you as spiritual, but carnal." They outstripped other churches in gifts, yet they came short of other churches in grace. Such was the church of Laodicea: she was rich in gifts and poor in grace.

Now there are four cases wherein men may have strong gifts and yet but little grace:

When men's notions are clear and strong, but men's experiences and affections are low and weak. To have more expressions than impressions is to be like the moon that, though it grows big and increases to become full, yet increases only in light and not in heat. So men, when they merely increase in light of notions and speculations, and not in heat of affection towards God and in the practical part of Christianity (and, it is to be feared, much of the religion of these times is of this stamp), are more in notion than motion; more in talking than walking; more in parts than grace.

When your gifts are not influential upon your life. Look,

as it is in that disease called the rickets that children are liable to—they may grow big in the head and yet decay in the lower parts—so there are some (as has been shown) who have the disease of spiritual rickets. They grow big in the head, big in gifts, and yet decay in their vitals, decay in grace and in the exercise of it.

When their gifts tend to the promotion of division in the church and pride in their own hearts. This was discovered in the church of Corinth. They came behind in no gift; but see what Paul said in 1 Corinthians 1:11: "For it hath been declared unto me of you, my brethren, by them which are of the house of Chloe, that there are contentions among you." And then in verse 12: "Now this I say, that every one of you saith, 'I am of Paul,' 'I of Apollos,' 'I of Cephas,' and 'I of Christ'." They were carnal as to grace, and walked as men, though they were high in gifts. And when gifts engender strife in the church, and produce pride in a man's heart with vain and high conceits, this is an argument they are but mere gifts. The Corinthians were in everything enriched by God, in all utterance and in all knowledge, so that they came behind in no gift. They had an abundance of knowledge, but "knowledge puffeth up; charity edifieth" (1 Corinthians 8:1).

When gifts are increased merely by virtue of continual study and industry; when gifts proceed merely from strength of natural parts, advantaged by education, study and diligence. If gifts merely proceed from that fountain, there may be much gifts but little grace. The greatest scholars are not always the best men. The reason is that their gifts are gotten by industry and diligence; their gifts may be high when their graces are low.

The fifth premise is this: there are cases wherein men may decay and be weak in gifts, and yet may be said to have strength of grace.

If the case proceeds merely from a natural, not a sinful defect. If weak gifts proceed from sinful defects, it argues grace is but weak. If the weakness proceeds from negligence, from sloth, from carelessness to attend upon ordinances, from idleness in not reading, in not meditating, not praying, not using holy conference, then grace decays with gifts. These are sinful defects; but if weak gifts proceed merely from natural defects, as a man of a shallow capacity, of a slow speech, of a bad memory, of a weak body either through sickness or old age, the weakeness is because there are natural decays in the body; for the putting forth of gifts depends upon the temperature and disposition of the body. As it is with an instrument of music that is out of tune, which makes no melody though the instrument is good, so a body out of tune has not that use of or ability to develop gifts. It is the same with an old preacher: his gifts may decay when he is an old man so that he may not have such freedom of speech, such clearness of judgment, or such strength of memory as the body decays. The gift of elocution will decay, and his memory may decay, so that he shall not be so ready in delivering the Word, but yet he may have as great ability in preaching, yea, more experience, more solid judgment, and more clear understanding in the mysteries of the gospel than a young man can have.

So it is with Christians: their gifts may decay, as the temper of the body decays. It is just as with a musician: when he is a young man, his joints being more pliable, he plays more nimbly and melodiously upon an instrument of music; but when he comes to be an old man, he cannot play so nimbly and melodiously; his joints are stiff, but yet he has more skill than a young man has. When this does not proceed from sinful defects, but from natural defects, then may a man's grace be strong though his gifts and parts are weak.

If you lack those external advantages to further and promote the growth of gifts. For example, a Christian who follows an ordinary trade, who carries a water tank on his shoulders, may attain more brokenness of heart, more humility and self-denial, more experience of the goodness of God toward his soul, and of the method of God, than he who perhaps is in some great, honorable, and eminent employment. But that Christian who has this mean and small employment, and such poor education, shall not attain those gifts that others have attained who have greater advantages. In the case of a scholar who has external advantages, such as education and literature, his gifts and parts may be much increased, while perhaps a poor man who follows the plow may attain to more grace and acquaintance with the ways of God. Now if such a man has not so many gifts as others, it is not his sin; God does not require more than He gives.

If you have not a calling to use or put forth the exercise of your gifts. Your gifts may decay, though grace does not decay. Gifts are increased by exercise; the less they are exercised, the more they decay. If you have not an opportunity to exercise your gifts as in former times you had, in such case a Christian who is strong in grace may grow weaker in gifts.

If what you want in gifts you make up in humility. Strength of grace is not to be measured by notions and speculations in the head, but by humility in the heart; therefore though your gifts are weak, if your humility be great, you have strength of grace. The fewer blossoms there are on the branches, the more sap there is in the root. He who has great parts and is proud of them, it is much to be feared, has less grace than that man who has but few gifts and low parts, but, in the sense of his own weakness, has low and self-denying thoughts of himself.

Last, if what you want in gifts you make up in your practice by a holy and conscionable walking. That martyr who said, "I cannot dispute, but I can burn for the truth," had more grace than those who could dispute and not burn.

The application of this case is only for caution, and I shall give you a threefold caution.

CAUTION 1. Take heed you are not proud of the greatest measure of gifts you have. There is nothing in the world that a man is so apt to be proud of as his gifts. A man is not so apt to be so proud of grace because he has a principle to check his pride, but he is apt to be proud of his gifts. A man is not apt to be proud of outward endowments, such as clothing, riches, and the like, as he is apt to be proud of gifts. Expositors who handle the prophecy of Ezekiel say that Ezekiel is called "Thou son of man" 93 times in that prophecy. Now there is no other prophet mentioned in all the Bible but one who is called "the son of man," and that is Daniel. Expositors give this reason why Ezekiel is called by this title: because he was a prophet of the greatest gifts, and had the most glorious visions of all the prophets. Compare this prophecy with Isaiah,

Jeremiah, Daniel, Hosea, or all the rest; yet Ezekiel's prophecy is a more dark, mysterious, and profound book. Now Ezekiel being a prophet of the greatest gifts, God took this care to keep his heart low: "Thou son of man, Thou son of man." And all is to keep his heart low, which teaches us that those who have great gifts ought to spend a great deal of time keeping their hearts humble and low, because there is a flatulent humor in our nature whereby we are apt to swell and be raised up in the sense of our own gifts.

CAUTION 2. Prize a little grace before a great measure of gifts. You will prize a pearl, though it is no bigger than a pea, more than a great heap of stones. There is great reason why we should prize a little grace before much gifts:

Grace will last when gifts are withering. Blazing comets will fall when the star never falls; a falling star is no star, but only a comet. So hypocrites may have a great blaze of their gifts, and yet may fall like comets that hover in the air. Grace is like a star that keeps fixed in its orbit. There is a great deal of difference between a painted face and a natural complexion; the painted face will not always last, but a natural complexion will always remain. Gifts are but paint, the ornament of the creature; but true grace, which is as the natural complexion, will remain.

Prize a little grace before much gifts, because gifts will leave you short of heaven. Christ told the learned scribe that he was "not far from the kingdom of heaven"; but alas, for all his gifts and learning, he fell short of heaven. "Many will say to Me (said Christ) in that day, 'Lord, Lord, have not we prophesied in Thy name, and in Thy name cast out devils, and in Thy name done many wondrous works?' " (Matthew 7:22). You see, it is observable that these men might pretend to high and great gifts, and yet against these men, to whom God opened the secrets of His kingdom, He shut the gates of heaven. A man may be a preacher, and have the secrets of heaven opened to him, and yet have the gates of heaven shut against him. A man may attain the gift in Christ's name to cast out devils, a great and miraculous gift, and yet those men who cast *out* devils were themselves cast *to* devils. "We have done many wondrous works." They who did wonders were made a wonder; they who had so many gifts came short of heaven; yea, they who preach to others may themselves be cast away.

CAUTION 3. Do not mistake strength of gifts to be strength of grace. Parents would not judge their children strong when their heads and breasts are big and their feet but feeble. So you may grow big in your heads, in notions, in speculations, and in gifts, and yet be feeble in the practice of grace.

Now, that you may not mistake yourselves and be deceived, I'll show you how you may know the difference between those who have strong gifts and those who have strong grace. In general take this: as art resembles nature, so gifts resemble grace. But there are four differences.

First, as grace strengthens, corruption weakens. It is with grace and lusts as it was with the house of Saul and the house of David. As David's house grew stronger and stronger, so Saul's house grew weaker and weaker. As the ark was set up, Dagon was thrown down; the Dagon of corruption will be thrown down before the ark of grace and the ark of the covenant;

but gifts may strengthen, and yet corruption never be weaker. Indeed, gifts discover corruption, but are not able to mortify and subdue it. Gifts discover many corruptions, but mortify none. Gifts take a cognizance of many a sin, but never put a period to any.

Men who have gifts resemble the moon, and men who have grace resemble the sun. The moon has an influence upon the water to make it move, to make it ebb and flow, and the moon sheds light upon all creatures, but it has no heat to make those creatures grow and spring. So a man of gifts may have light, but not heat in those gifts to make grace to grow and sin to fade and wither. Gracious men are like the sun that not only gives light but heat; by the influence thereof things spring and grow out of the earth. The great parts of a gifted man often strengthen his corruptions, but do not weaken them. Augustine could say, "Ignorant and illiterate men take heaven, when others with all their scholarship go to hell."

Second, where there is strength of grace, there the heart is more humbled under the measures of grace received. The stronger the graces are, the more the heart is humbled. But strength of parts in most men makes them proud and lofty. Empty vessels make the greatest noise, and so do shallow streams. So men who have great gifts are often empty of grace (1 Corinthians 8:1). They who have more gifts than grace are puffed up with pride; by the humility of the soul you may know whether that soul is stronger in grace than in gifts.

Third, the man with strength of grace looks more after the supply of the grace he wants than feels contentment in the grace he has. Thus argued Paul: he had more grace when he thus spoke: "I do strive after more and more grace, if by any means I might attain the resurrection of the dead." That is, "I labor after perfection of grace, which those shall have who are raised from the dead and exalted in heaven." But now a man who has gifts is more apt to look to what he has than what he lacks. Men of gifts are apt to look upon their gifts in a multiplying glass (seeing them as more than they are) and upon their failings in an extenuating glass as less than they are.

Fourth, the more grace any one has, the more he labors that others may be partakers of the same grace. When the Apostle Peter speaks of the duties of husbands and wives, he would have them further one another in the way to heaven, "considering they are heirs together of the grace of God" (1 Peter 3:7). Christ also spoke to Peter: "when thou art converted, strengthen thy brethren" (Luke 22:32). By conversion is not meant God's first act in bringing Peter's soul home to Christ, but an establishing work of grace, as if Christ should have said, "Peter, now your grace is weak and it will be weaker by your fall, but when you have recovered from your fall, and the denial of your Master, then strengthen your brethren; labor to strengthen the graces of other men when your graces are strong and your strength recovered."

And this is a very good evidence that you have not only grace, but strength of grace yourself, when you are careful to strengthen others. But such as have gifts only, with little or no grace, are loath to communicate their gifts to others. They would willingly monopolize their gifts, and begrudge imparting them to others. They do not desire that other men have the like gifts as themselves, lest their glory should be darkened. They are not of John the Baptist's mind, who cared not if he decreased, so long as Christ increased. Rather they are like one Aspendius, a skillful musician who would never play on his instrument before any of his profession, lest they should learn his skill.

This is a notable means to discover whether you have strong grace or strong gifts only, which you may know by your willingness and readiness to communicate unto others what God has imparted unto you.

Sermon 13

"Be strong in the grace of God, which is in Christ Jesus." 2 Timothy 2:1

You have heard the first doctrine opened: believers are not to be satisfied in weak measures of grace already received, but ought to endeavor to attain greater strength of grace. I shall now proceed to the improvement of this point by making some application. I shall direct the use to two sorts of Christians: first, to such as are weak in the faith; second, to such as are strong and grown Christians.

With weak believers I would leave these directions and consolations:

1. It is your wisdom to look more after the truth of your grace than the measure of it. It is an error in many Christians, especially young converts, that they bring their graces to the balance rather than to the touchstone. They *weigh* them when they should *try* them. Peter was asked by Christ: "Simon, lovest thou Me more than these?" He answered not about the measure of his love, but about the truth of his love: "Lord, I love Thee, and Thou knowest I love Thee." It is not the quantity or measure, but the nature and essence of grace which is of primary consideration. If you have grace in truth and reality, it will increase. Be sure your grace is right, and as the light shines more and more to the perfect day, and as the nature of leaven is that it spreads through the whole lump, so is grace. It is of a

spreading and increasing nature; and therefore be careful that your grace, for nature, for essence, and for the measure, is true; and then it will increase.

2. In finding out the truth of grace, we must not measure it so much by actions as affections and holy dispositions of the heart. The bent, frame, and tendencies of the heart are the best revealers of grace in the heart. When a Christian casts up all the stock of grace he has, he will find that it consists more in desires than in endeavors, and more in endeavors and attempts to perform holy duties than in the performance itself. Natural life is more discernible by the heat than by the color. A painter may counterfeit the one, but not the other. When the Lord Jesus described the beauty of His spouse, He did not say, "How fair are your looks!" but "How fair is your love!" (Song of Solomon 4:10).

3. Be not discouraged though men of glorious gifts fall away, for the poorest Christians who have the smallest measure of grace shall never fall away. The gifts of a formalist may quickly wither, for they have their root in nature; but the graces of a true Christian shall never perish because they have their root in Christ. A Christian's life is hidden with Christ, hidden in Him as in a root, as in the fountain of life. A painted face may soon fade, but not a true and natural complexion. The varnish of a formal hypocrite is soon washed out, but when true grace, like a color in grain, has grown habitually in the soul, it is not removable. Sooner will the sun discard its own beams than Christ desert and destroy the least measure of true grace, which is a beam from that Sun of righteousness.

4. Improve your little grace well; this is the way to have more. "To him that hath shall it be given." That

is, more shall be given. God never gave any man a talent to hide it in a napkin. The least measure of grace must be accounted for.

Grace is improved when we ascribe all the glory of grace unto God. He spoke rightly who said, "Lord, thy pound hath gained ten pounds" (Luke 19:16). Thy pound, not my pains. We should do all to the praise of the glory of God's grace. If we give God the glory of His grace, He will give us the comfort and increase of our grace.

Grace is improved for the edification and building up of others in their most holy faith. To do good to others is the best way to get more good ourselves. The more the well is drawn, the more water comes and the better the water is; so the more your grace is exercised, the more grace you will have, and the sweeter will the comfort be of your grace.

5. You weak Christians, do not deny the truth of grace in your souls because you cannot find the strength of grace in your souls. A poor, weak man in a consumption cannot lift up such a weight, nor can he bear such a burden as a man in strength and health can do; yet he has life as well as the strongest man in the world. It may be day when it is not noon; you may, in respect of spiritual estate, have the strength of a child, though not the strength of a man. It is not only an act of unthankfulness to God, but also of uncharitableness to a man's own soul to conclude a nullity of grace from the weakness of it.

6. Look not so much on your sins, but look upon your grace also, though weak. Weak Christians look more on their sins than on their graces; yet God looks on their graces and overlooks their sins and infirmities.

The Holy Ghost said, "Ye have heard of the patience of Job" (James 5:11). He might also have said, "Ye have heard of the *im*patience of Job," but God reckons His people not by what is *bad* in them, but by what is *good* in them. Mention is made of Rahab's entertainment of the spies, but no mention is made that she told a lie when she did so. That which was well done is mentioned to her praise, and what was amiss is buried in silence, or, at least, is not recorded against her and charged upon her. He who drew the picture of Alexander, when he had a scar on his face, drew him with his finger on his scar. God lays the finger of mercy upon the scars of our sins. Oh, it is good serving such a Master, who is ready to reward the good we do and is ready to forgive and pass by what is amiss. Therefore, you who have but little grace, yet remember that God will have His eye on that little grace. He will not quench the smoking flax, nor break the bruised reed.

7. Learn this for your comfort: though you have but a little grace, yet that little grace shall not be extinguished by your strong corruption, but at last it shall overmaster your corruptions. It was said of Esau and Jacob: "The one shall be stronger than the other, and the elder shall serve the younger" (Genesis 25:23). And so it came to pass in the time of Jehoshaphat, when there was no king in Edom. That may be fitly applied to the affairs of the soul: the elder shall serve the younger. Corruption in the soul is older than grace in the soul, and corruption is so opposite to grace that it labors for the extinction of grace. But this spark shall live in the midst of the sea of corruption till at last that great deep shall be made dry; and the house of David shall at last quite put down the house of Saul. The

name of the Lord will perform this. And therefore, you who are but a weak Christian, learn to stay yourself on the name of the Lord till judgment is brought forth unto victory.

The second use of this doctrine is for strong believers, such as have attained to a higher form of grace in the school of Christ.

Though you are strong in grace, yet remember it is not the grace of God *in* you, but the free grace of God *towards* you by which you are justified. It is not our inherent righteousness, but the imputed righteousness of Jesus Christ that is our justification. Oh, consider, you who have most grace, what would become of you were it not for free grace? Free grace is the surest and only refuge for a soul to fly to. God can find matter of condemnation against you not only for your worst sins, but your best duties. The best Christian has no reason to venture his soul on the best thought that ever he conceived, not on the most holy duty ever he performed, not on the highest grace that ever he exercised.

Nehemiah, who had much grace and did much for God, His people, His house, and His cause, yet prayed after all this, "Spare me according to the greatness of Thy mercy," intimating that God might find matter enough to ruin him if God did not spare him for His mercy's sake. So Paul, in the discharge of his ministry, proceeded with so much uprightness that he spoke thus of himself: "I know nothing by myself, yet am I not hereby justified" (1 Corinthians 4:4). He knew that all the grace, excellency, and uprightness in him would not make him righteous in the sight of God. We read

HEZEKIA, "WE DON'T KNOW WHAT TO DO BUT OUR EYES ARE ON YOU."

that when Jehoshaphat had mustered up all his strength, which was very great, for he had eleven hundred thousand men in his militia, yet he went to God and prayed: "Lord, we have no might or power against these multitudes, and we know not what to do, only our eyes are up to Thee" (2 Chronicles 20:12). So when a Christian has mustered up all the strength of his grace, and considered the great power of his corruptions which set themselves against him, he had best go to God and say, "Lord, I have no power against these many and great corruptions, but my eyes are to Thy grace that Thou may help me."

GOD EMPOWERS GRACE, NOT MAN.

FAITH

In a compass, one foot is fixed in the center while the other turns about the circumference. So the soul must fix and stay itself on Christ while it is exercised about holy duties. Though Christ (as I formerly mentioned) commended many parts of the spouse, He did not commend her hands, to teach us that all the spouse could do could not make her amiable in the eyes of Christ; not the spouse's working for Christ, but Christ's work in the spouse made her beautiful. It is very hard through strength of grace to abound in the work of the Lord, and yet keep the heart humble.

And therefore consider that they who have most grace have great cause to be humbled, and that in many respects.

1. You have not as much grace and perfection as once you had. Once man was beautiful and bespangled with many glorious perfections before the fall; it might have been said of man that he "was perfect, as his heavenly Father was perfect" (cf. Matthew 5:48), for God made man upright, that is, perfect; nothing was wanting then to make man both a happy and holy

creature. But, alas, the image of God in us is now obliterated and defaced! *YES IF WE ARE UNREGENERATE* *NO! IF WE ARE TRANSFORMED!*

2. He who has the most grace has not as much as he shall have in heaven. "Not that I am perfect already, but I forget those things that are behind, and I press forward unto those things that are before, yea, I press towards the mark for the prize of the high calling of God in Christ Jesus" (Philippians 3:12–14). We read under the law several things that were to be a cubit and a half high and broad, the cubit being an imperfect measure. It was to note that no man in this life has an exactness and perfection; and the uttermost that is attainable by us in this life is but imperfect. In this life there is a *plus ultra*, something still to be attained in religion; but in heaven men shall be perfect. We shall in heaven be like Jesus Christ, whom though we now see but darkly and in a glass, then we shall see Him as He is.

3. They who have much grace should yet be humbled, for there are those who have more grace than you, and yet have had less time and fewer advantages than you. There are those who have gone before you as far as strength of grace, and yet have come behind you as far as means of grace. There are those who were the last, and are first and before you.

4. Be humbled under much grace, for you have not as much grace as you should have had considering the means of grace you have lived under. How many years have you been in the school of Christ, and yet what little proportionate progress have you made in the knowledge of Jesus Christ! We may all blush to think what dunces we have been in this school of Christ! The trees of the garden should bear more fruit than the

trees of the forest. The fig tree therefore, which was unfruitful, was the more intolerable because it was in the garden, in the vineyard. What the Apostle complains of the Hebrews, we may justly take up against ourselves, that "for the time we ought to have been teachers, and yet have need that one teach us again what are the first principles of the oracles of God, and are become such as have need of milk, and not of strong meat" (Hebrews 5:12).

5. They who have much grace, and are strong in grace, yet have cause to be humble because it is likely that they had more grace and did more good heretofore than now. And who is there who is not decayed, who has not, in some degree or other, "left their first love"? Have you not had (I speak to grown and experienced Christians) more love and zeal for God, more hatred of sin, more grief for sin, more fear of offending God than now you have? Are there not many who have and express less desire after duty, less fervency, less frequency, less delight in holy duties than formerly? Alas, how many, through pride and spiritual improvidence, through neglect of ordinances and wordly-mindedness, have much abated in their spiritual estate!

6. Be humbled that, though you are strong in grace, yet you have many corruptions in you more strong than many graces. More are our vain thoughts than our meditations, and more are the things we are ignorant of than the things we know. Corruption is strong enough to keep grace low, but the best grace is not strong enough to bring corruption under. When we would do good, evil is present and powerful with us to hinder us from doing good; but when we are doing

evil, good is not present to hinder us from that evil. We are more in sinning than in obeying. Our corruptions are like Goliath, our graces like David. We exercise more kinds of sins than graces. As in a field there are more briars and thorns than useful trees, and in a garden there are more unprofitable weeds than roses and lilies, so in the souls of the best there are swarms of vain, earthly, and sinful thoughts when there are but very few holy and heavenly thoughts.

7. Another argument why strong Christians should be humble is that, though they may have grace, yet they are subject to fall into that sin which is most contrary to the grace wherein they are most eminent. Abraham was most eminent for faith. He is said to be "strong in faith." He is called "the father of the faithful." Those who are of faith are "blessed with faithful Abraham." And yet, for all this, Abraham fell into distrust of God's providence and power when he spoke untruthfully and denied his wife.

Job was renowned for his patience. "You have heard of the patience of Job," said James, and yet we read in the story of Job's trial that his impatience broke out in many rash speeches and wishes.

Moses was eminently meek "above all the men which were upon the face of the earth." And yet it is said of him that "his spirit was provoked, so that he spake unadvisedly with his lips." And you shall find meek Moses thus expostulating with God Himself: "I am not able to bear all this people alone, because it is too heavy for me; and if Thou deal thus with me, kill me, I pray Thee, out of hand, if I have found favor in Thine eyes; and let me not see my wretchedness" (Numbers 11:15).

8. This further consideration may also humble us: in the highest and greatest exercise of grace there is much mixture of sin. We may observe that even those good actions, for which many of the people of God are recorded in Scripture, are yet blemished with some notable defect. Rahab's faith in entertaining the spies was blemished with her failing in telling a lie concerning them. It was also good the midwives did, when they refused to obey the bloody decree of the king of Egypt and would not kill the male children of the Hebrews, and yet they miscarried (as some observe) in their answer to the king when they made their excuse. We are apt to mingle sin with the best actions we do, and so are apt to plow with an ox and an ass. And our corruptions are apt to reveal themselves even while we are upon the exercise of our graces.

Let the strong labor to be more strong so that they may be "strengthened with all might, according to His glorious power, unto all patience and longsuffering with joyfulness" (Colossians 1:11). And therefore it is that the Apostle prayed for the Romans, that they might be filled by the God of hope, "with all joy and peace in believing, that you might abound in hope through the power of the Holy Ghost" (Romans 15:13). And yet, in the next verse he told them: "I myself am persuaded of you, my brethren, that ye are full of goodness and that ye are filled with all knowledge." And as he prayed for the Romans, upon the same terms he pressed the Thessalonians, of whom he said, "Now as touching brotherly love, ye need not that I write unto you, for ye yourselves are taught of God to love one another. And indeed you do it towards all the brethen which are in all Macedonia; but we beseech you, brethren, that ye increase more and more." Job said, "The righteous shall hold on his way, and he that hath clean hands shall be stronger and stronger" (Job 17:9).

To quicken you hereunto, consider that the more grace we have on earth, the more glory we shall have in heaven. As God unequally dispenses His gifts in this life, so accordingly He crowns. There are degrees of torments in hell. The hypocritical scribes and Pharisees, who devoured widows' houses and for a pretense made long prayers, are doomed by Christ Himself to have greater damnation. And that servant who knew his Lord's will and prepared not himself, neither did according to His will, shall be beaten with many stripes. Now, if there are different degrees of torment in hell, then, surely, there are different degrees of glory in heaven, and those according to different degrees of grace here on earth. *No! But according to rewards!*

It is of the nature of grace to grow and increase. And therefore, if you have grace, either in the truth of it or in the strength of it, it will certainly grow. Grace in Scripture is compared to a grain of mustard seed, the least of seeds, which afterwards sprouts and springs so that it becomes the largest of plants. In the same chapter (Matthew 13), grace is compared unto leaven which, being put into the heap of meal, "leaveneth the whole lump." So grace, as I noted before, in the heart is of a spreading nature and will diffuse itself into all the parts, powers, and faculties of soul and body. Christians are, therefore, compared to the branches of a vine which, of all trees, grows most and brings forth the most fruit. A picture does not grow, but a living child will.

Faith not Grace

Faith

Such as are strong Christians should yet grow more and more, because in this world there is no limit and measure set for spiritual growth. The goal for a Christian is this: he must grow in grace till his head reaches up to heaven, till grace is perfected in glory.

Shall worldlings set no bounds to their desires after wealth and land, and yet will you take up with poor measures of grace for religion? The ordinary answer of ignorant people is: "What, must we be wiser than our forefathers were?" And those who have great wealth left them by their forefathers are not satisfied with it unless they increase their estate. Let this shame the slothfulness and supine negligence of many who content themselves with measures of grace.

Last, consider, as for those who were eminent for grace, in what esteem they were in the church of God, and with what honorable mention they are recorded in the Word of God! Such are remembered to be of note in the church of God. See what a eulogy the Holy Ghost gives Job: "There was none like him in the earth" (Job 1:8). God loves those who are singularly and excellently good; an ordinary performance does not so please Him. He asks, "What do you more than others?"

Solomon was so renowned for wisdom that it is said that "amongst many nations there was no king like him," that is, for wisdom. So Hezekiah was eminent for trusting in God, who feared not to break in pieces the brazen serpent, but trusted in God: "None like him of all the kings of Judah" (2 Kings 18:5). And so eminent was the zeal of good Josiah after a thorough reformation that he is also crowned with this commendation: "And like him was there no king before him, that turned to the Lord with all his heart, and with all his soul, and all his might" (2 Kings 23:25).

By all these instances it is clear what honorable esteem the eminent, particular graces of God's servants have had in the sight of the Lord.

Sermon 14

"Be strong in the grace of God, which is in Christ Jesus." 2 Timothy 2:1

Having in the last foregoing sermons treated grace in its strength and growth, I am now going to speak to this additional clause in the text: "Which is in Christ Jesus." This passage is here inserted by the Apostle that he might let Timothy know to whom he was beholden for all the grace he had received, even unto Jesus Christ. In the tenth verse he speaks of salvation "that is in Christ Jesus," and here of grace that "is in Christ Jesus," to note: (1) that Jesus Christ is the fountain and foundation both of grace and glory. Jesus Christ gives grace and Jesus Christ also gives "salvation with eternal glory" (verse 10); (2) that those who receive grace from Christ Jesus shall also receive salvation by Him, for there is an inseparable union between grace and glory. "The grace of God that is in Christ Jesus." Grace may be said to be in Christ as He is a subject recipient, and so Christ is said to be "full of grace and truth." He had the "Spirit without measure," and "it pleased the Father that in Him all fullness should dwell" (Colossians 1:19). In Christ Jesus, there is a fountain redundant, overflowing, and ever-flowing to His people, for "of His fullness we receive grace for grace" (John 1:16). *Yes! Not weak grace or strong grace!*

Again, when it is said that grace is in Christ Jesus, we must consider Christ, first, as God co-essential with

1 to 1

1:1
ratio

the Father, and He is the author and giver of grace, and of every good and perfect gift. Second, consider Him as a Mediator, "God-man," and so He is the purchaser and procurer of grace, and of all the blessings of the new covenant, for "the blessing of Abraham cometh upon the Gentiles through Christ Jesus" (Galatians 3:14).

There are three things implied by this phrase, "in Christ Jesus."

1. Jesus Christ is the author and giver of grace. He only is the author and finisher of faith, and of every grace in His people.   *FAITH NO GRACE, GRACE IS COMPLETE.*

2. Christ is the purchaser of grace, so that all the grace that is bestowed upon us by God is through Christ and for His sake. Grace is from Christ as a fountain, and by Christ as a conduit.

3. Christ is the preserver of grace. All the grace that is in us is in Christ Jesus. He keeps all our graces for us just as the beams of the sun are preserved by their union with the sun. "Our life is hid with Christ in God" (Colossians 3:3), hidden as the life of a tree is hidden in the root and the being of a stream is hidden in the fountain. And herein is the comfort of believers. Their condition is more stable, immutable, and safe than Adam's ever was in innocence; for he had all perfections of a creature, but they were in his own keeping. But now, all the grace that is in a believer is in Christ Jesus, *by* whom and *in* whom grace is safely preserved so that it shall never perish.

DOCTRINE. All the measures of grace whereby believers are partakers, they receive them in and from Jesus Christ.

In the handling of this point, I will thus proceed,

first, to show you the truth of it and, second, give you the reasons and grounds of it. Now to prove that all grace is received in and through Christ, I will show you the truth of this:

1. By many resemblances to which Christ is compared in the Scripture.

2. By many types of Christ in the Old Testament.

3. By many express testimonies in the New Testament concerning this truth.

1. There are many resemblances in Scripture which illustrate that all grace is from Christ Jesus.

He is compared to a root. He is called the root of Jesse not only because He came of the stock of David, but because He gives grace to Jew and Gentile who believe, for "to Him shall the Gentiles seek," as it follows in the next words (Romans 15:12). Now, that the prophet there speaks of Christ is plain by the Apostle's express application of that prophecy unto Christ, calling Him the root of Jesse in whom the Gentiles should trust. And Christ speaks of Himself: "I am the vine; as the branch cannot bear fruit of itself, except it abide in the vine, no more can ye, except ye abide in Me" (John 15:4). The life, sap, nourishment, growth, and fruitfulness of a branch are altogether from the root, with which the branches have union and communion.

Christ is called the Head of His people. "He is the Head of the body, the church" (Colossians 1:18). Now, as sense and motion are derived from the head to the members of the body, so also grace is derived from Jesus Christ to every true believer, every living member of His body.

Christ is called the "Sun of righteousness," because

as heat and light are communicated by the sun to things here below, so there is a sweet influence of grace from Christ upon believers. As by virtue of the sun's influence the vegetable and sensible creatures live, move, and grow, so also the life and growth of grace in the soul are from that divine influence which Jesus Christ sheds upon believers.

Christ is compared to a fountain, even "a fountain opened to the house of David, and to the inhabitants of Jerusalem, for sin and for uncleanness" (Zechariah 13:1). So that as water streams forth in the river from the fountain, so grace flows down from Jesus Christ, who is a fountain, upon believers, where all fullness of grace forever dwells and from whence all grace is drawn and derived. This is the first proof.

2. This truth may be demonstrated by the many types of Christ in the Old Testament, which fore-shadowed unto us that all grace is from Jesus Christ.

Aaron the High Priest was to lay his hands on the people and bless them. And herein he was a type of Christ, our great and heavenly High Priest, through whom we are blessed with all grace. God has "blessed us with all spiritual blessings in heavenly places in Christ" (Ephesians 1:3). Jesus Christ is sent by God to bless His people and "to turn every one of them from their iniquities" (Acts 3:26). And therefore, it is recorded by St. Luke that a little before the ascension of our blessed Savior He laid His hands on His disciples and blessed them. And so He still blesses all true believers with the spiritual blessing of grace.

Another type of Christ was Joseph, who in many ways was the most beloved of his father's children. So Jesus Christ was the Son of His Father's love. Joseph was hated by his brethren and sold for twenty pieces of silver. So was Jesus Christ. "He came unto His own and His own received Him not" (John 1:11). He was rejected by them and sold for thirty pieces of silver. Joseph was carried into Egypt, and so persecution drove Christ into Egypt immediately after He was born. Joseph was falsely accused and condemned; so was Christ. Joseph's troubles ended in his advancement; so all the troubles of Christ "wrought for Him a far more exceeding and eternal weight of glory—God having therefore highly exalted Him and given Him a name above every name." For now Christ is set down at the right hand of the Father. But especially in this did Joseph typify Christ, that in that dreadful, lasting famine in Egypt Joseph had the custody of all the corn in the land. He had the issuing out of all provision for bread in all the land of Egypt. So the Lord Jesus is the Lord-keeper of all that store of grace with which believers are furnished, which grace is given to help them in time of need. Jesus Christ has the key of David; He has the key of the treasury of grace.

Another type of Jesus Christ was Joshua, who gave to Israel entrance and possession of the good land of Canaan, and all the promised blessings of it. So Jesus Christ gives to His people better things than the milk and Canaan. "He will give grace and glory, and no good thing will He withhold from them that walk uprightly" (Psalm 84:11). Our Jesus gives His people a better rest than ever Joshua brought to Israel.

Another type of Christ was the candlestick of the tabernacle, the seven lamps whereof gave light to the whole tabernacle. Now what did these seven lamps typify but the graces of the Spirit of Christ? For so it is said that there were "seven lamps of fire burning before the throne, which are the seven spirits of God." The Holy Ghost, and the graces of it, are so represented by seven spirits in this regard because of the variety and protection of that grace which is in the Lord Jesus, and by His Spirit communicated to all His members.

3. The third proof of this doctrine may be drawn from the consideration of those clear testimonies of this truth in the New Testament. St. John speaks thus of Christ, that "of His fullness we have all received, and grace for grace" (John 1:16). In Christ there is not only plenty but bounty; not only an abundance of grace but a redundance of grace. Christians have the fullness of a vessel, but Christ has the fullness of a fountain. Take a drop of water out of a vessel and it is not as full as before, but draw as much water as you please out of the well of the water of life and there is no lack of water. From Christ we receive grace for grace, that is, say some, the grace of the New Testament added to the grace that was revealed under the Old Testament. Or "grace for grace," say others, means a perfection of grace according to the perfection that is in Christ. As in a natural generation, the child receives from his father limb for limb and part for part, so, in this spiritual regeneration, Jesus Christ, the everlasting Father, gives grace for grace. Or you may understand by this expression, "grace for grace," that Jesus Christ is not only the author of grace, but gives grace for grace, that is, one grace after another, grace upon grace. The being of grace and the increase of grace are both from Christ.

It also appears that Christ is the author and bestower of all grace by that ordinary prayer wherewith

[handwritten margin note: 1:1 FULLNESS OF CHRIST'S GRACE IN US!]

the Apostle usually closes all his epistles: "The grace of our Lord Jesus Christ be with you all." We have the same prayer to the Romans and to the Galatians: "Brethren, the grace of our Lord Jesus Christ be with your spirit." It is also in the close of the epistles to the Philippians, Thessalonians, and to Timothy: "Grace be with thee, Amen." All this to note that Jesus Christ is the fountain from whence, and the conduit by whom, all grace is conveyed unto believers. As, in the vision that the prophet Zechariah saw, there were "two olive branches, which through the golden pipes did empty the golden oil out of themselves" (Zechariah 4:12), so Jesus Christ, that true olive tree, drops and distills grace upon His church whereby they receive from His fullness grace for grace.

OBJECTION. But in giving this honor unto Christ, do you not derogate from God the Father by saying that all grace is from Christ?

ANSWER 1. It is no derogation to God the Father to ascribe this unto Christ because it pleased the Father that in Him should all fullness dwell.

ANSWER 2. And besides, Christ and the Father are one. In saying all grace is from Christ, we are also saying that all is from the Father too; and in saying it is from the Father, we are saying it is from Christ too. And therefore is this ordinary prayer prefixed to the beginning of most of the epistles: "Grace be unto you from God the Father and from our Lord Jesus Christ." So that in the subscription and in the inscription of each epistle, grace is ascribed to God the Son, but not so as to exclude God the Father, and to God the Father but so as not to exclude God the Son.

ANSWER 3. And then again, Jesus Christ is com-

missioned and designed by the Father to give out grace
to His people, for Christ speaks of Himself: "I came
down from heaven, not to do Mine own will, but the
will of Him that sent Me" (John 6:38). Now it is the will
of God that from Christ believers should receive both
justifying and sanctifying grace. Our sanctification is
God's will, and Christ came to fulfill that will of God.
So speaks the Apostle: "Sacrifice and offering, and
burnt-offerings, and offering for sin Thou wouldst not,
neither hadst pleasure therein; then said I, 'Lo, I come
to do Thy will, O God'—by which will we are sanctified,
through the offering of the body of Jesus Christ once
for all" (Hebrews 10:5–10). So the will of God the
Father and the will of Jesus Christ are the same in the
bestowing of grace. Jesus Christ received commission
from God the Father to bestow grace upon His people,
and will you see how that commission runs? You shall
find it in the prophet Isaiah: "The Spirit of the Lord
God is upon Me, because the Lord hath anointed Me
to bind up the broken-hearted, to proclaim liberty to
the captives, and the opening of the prison to them
that are bound" (Isaiah 61:1). Christ had a commission
under His Father's hand and seal, for "Him hath the
Father sealed" (John 6:27). Joseph received authority
from Pharaoh, and it was no dishonor to Pharaoh that
Joseph was commissioned to issue out all the stores of
corn to the Egyptians in the time of that famine. No
more is it any dishonor to the Father that Jesus Christ
bestows and conveys grace upon believers.

QUESTION. But does this not put the Spirit out of
office, who is called the Holy Spirit and the Spirit of
grace, because He works grace and holiness in the
hearts of the people of God?

ANSWER 1. What Christ is said to work, that the Holy Spirit also does, because by the Spirit of God Christ works. It is a good rule that the works of the blessed Trinity are undivided. All those works which are external, and relative to the creature, such as to create, preserve, redeem, and sanctify, are in respect of those things wrought equally common to all the Persons of the blessed Trinity. So we may say that whatever things the Father does the Son does likewise, and those things the Holy Ghost does also.

The work of sanctification is equally ascribed unto all the Persons. God the Father sanctifies His people. God the Son sanctifies His members, for He is their sanctification. He loved the church and gave Himself for it that He might sanctify and cleanse it with the washing of water through the Word; and yet the work of sanctification is most frequently ascribed to the Holy Ghost—goodness, righteousness, and truth. And indeed, all grace is called the "fruit of the Spirit," and the Spirit is called "the Spirit of grace and supplication," and "the Spirit of holiness and sanctification."

So our regeneration is ascribed to God the Father: "Blessed be the God and Father of our Lord Jesus Christ, who according to His abundant mercy hath begotten us again to a lively hope" (1 Peter 1:3). And so also we are the children of Christ by regeneration, for in this respect Christ is called the Father of eternity. "Behold," said the prophet in the name of Christ, "I and the children which Thou hast given me" (Isaiah 8:18). And that the prophet is speaking of Christ is clear from the application of these words to Him in the epistle to the Hebrews (2:13).

Neither is the Holy Ghost excluded from this working of grace and regeneration in us, for Christ told Nicodemus that "except a man be born again, except a man be born of water and the Spirit, he cannot enter the Kingdom of God" (John 3:3, 5). So it is said that God the Father blessed Abraham, and yet the blessing of Abraham came upon the Gentiles through Christ that they might receive the promise of the Spirit. By all which instances it appears that though there are diversities of gifts, yet the same Spirit; and though there are differences of administrations, yet the same Lord Jesus Christ, the author of all grace, through the Holy Spirit.

ANSWER 2. The reason and ground why Jesus Christ is the author, purchaser, and conveyor of grace to His people is:

1. Because God the Father has appointed Jesus Christ as Mediator to transact the great work of sanctifying and saving His elect.

2. Because by this the reproach shall be rolled away from Christ who, in His lifetime, was reputed the greatest of all malefactors and accordingly suffered death. They were wont to say, "Can any good come out of Nazareth?" (John 1:46). God has therefore given Him a name above all names so that He should not only be anointed with oil above His fellows, by His receiving the Spirit without measure, but also that the oil that was poured upon the head of our High Priest should run down upon the skirts of His garments, and that grace which was abundant in Him should also be redundant to His church, and run down and diffuse itself to all His members.

3. To manifest that Jesus Christ was the second Adam, and came into the world to repair the breaches

which the sin of the first Adam had made. By the fall, we not only contracted upon ourselves the guilt of Adam's sin, which to take off we need the righteousness of Christ imputed, but we have drawn upon ourselves the filthiness and pollution of sin. To take away the power of that, only the grace, holiness, and inherent righteousness of Christ imputed to us avail, and as the first Adam was the author and conveyor of the guilt, filthiness, and punishment of sin to his posterity, so Jesus Christ, the second Adam, conveys the life of grace into all His. As the first Adam was the author to communicate natural life, as he was made a living soul, so the second Adam communicated the spiritual life of grace as He was made a quickening Spirit. From the first Adam, by natural regeneration and propagation, we receive corruption for corruption; so from the second Adam we receive grace for grace.

USE. This doctrine confutes:

1. The error of the Socinians who say that all grace in Christ, whether His active or passive righteousness, was only to qualify His person and to merit His glorification without any reference to us unless as an example or pattern. But this opinion is sufficiently confuted by this doctrine, by which it has been shown that as all our grace is from Christ, so that abundance of grace that is in Christ is for us. As the woman has abundance of milk in her breast, not for herself but for her child, and the sun has abundance of light, not for itself but for the world, so Jesus Christ is full of grace and truth, but this fullness is for the purpose of the filling of His members. In the natural body there are some special parts that stand as officers to all the rest. The stomach

receives meat, not for itself but that it might communicate it to all the members. The head has the senses seated in it, not for itself but for the whole body. So it is in the mystical body whereof Christ is the Head. The abundance of grace which is treasured up in Christ is in order to supply every member with grace. "For their sakes," said Christ Himself of His elect, "I sanctify Myself, that they might also be sanctified through the truth" (John 17:19). Some refer this to Christ, being set apart to the office of Mediator, that it was not for His own sake, but for the sake of His members. And though there is grace enough in Christ to qualify His person, yet also there is grace enough in Him to justify our persons too, and sanctify our natures.

2. This also reproves the error, pride, and folly of the Pelagians, papists, and Arminians, who derogate from God and arrogate to themselves. These people, like Samson, have lost their spiritual strength, but do not and will not know that it is departed from them. They are poor and yet are proud, and while they are setting up the praise of nature, they prove themselves the enemies of grace. Alas! While they boast of a free will, they have cause to bewail a "servile will," as Luther calls it. It is true, man, by the fall, did not lose the faculty itself, but he has lost the rectitude of it. And yet proud man will be like the spider, spinning out a thread of his own, and thinking to climb up to heaven by threads spun out of his own bowels. But let such who rejoice in this fiction take heed at last that their hope is not cut off, and that their trust does not become like a spider's web.

Alas! Poor, proud wretch! Who made you to differ? Grevincovius, the Arminian, made this proud answer

to the Apostle's question: "I myself made myself to differ." This is divinity much like that of the heathens.
Seneca said, "That we live is of God, but that we live
well is of ourselves." And Cicero has also this saying,
and he tells us that it is the judgment of all men that
prosperity and success is from God, and must be
sought of God, but wisdom is gotten by ourselves. This
gave Augustine occasion to pass this censure on him,
"Cicero, in endeavoring to make men free, made them
sacrilegious." But let us take heed of this proud leaven
of Arminianism and learn from hence to be convinced
of the emptiness and insufficiency of our nature to
perform any supernatural good. For, alas! we are not
sufficient of ourselves to think anything as of ourselves,
but our sufficiency is from God. We have no grace but
what we receive from Christ. And grace is in no way
grace unless it is in every way free. We have little
reason to boast of the freedom of our will to do
anything that is spiritually good, because our will is not
free till it is by grace made free. We have no power to
become the sons of God till it is given to us to believe
on His name. And such are born not of the flesh, nor
of the will of man, but of God.

Sermon 15

"Be strong in the grace of God, which is in Christ Jesus." 2 Timothy 2:1

From the last clause in the text, "the grace of God which is in Christ Jesus," we have gathered this observation: All those measures of grace whereof believers are partakers they receive in and from Jesus Christ.

That this is so we have proved not only by the types of the Old Testament, but also by the express testimony of the New Testament, and have also given the grounds and reasons of this point, with some application, by way of reproof and confutation of the Arminian and Socinian errors. It remains to make some further application of this point, and so conclude the whole discourse.

USE OF EXHORTATION.

1. Do you receive all your grace from Jesus Christ? Then labor to be humble in the acknowledgment of this. Let the consideration and conscientious application of this doctrine quell all boasting in us of any excellency received. Our wisdom, righteousness, sanctification, and redemption are all from Christ, and therefore he that glories, let him glory in the Lord. "Consider, who made you to differ from another? And what have you that you did not receive? Now, if you did not receive it, why do you glory as if you had not received it?" (1 Corinthians 4:7). Who but a proud fool would magnify himself in that which either another

gave him or another had done for him? We count it an odious pride and folly in a man to boast himself of that which another has done. And therefore the Apostle professes that he did not carry himself as those false teachers had done who were crept into the church at Corinth: "We do not boast of things beyond our measure, that is, of other men's labors, nor boast in another man's line of things, made ready to our hand" (2 Corinthians 10:15–16). Now all grace is made ready to our hands, and is only the work of Jesus Christ in us who works all our works for us.

Ammianus Marcellinus tells us of one Lampadius, a great person in Rome, who, in all parts of the city, where other men had bestowed cost in building, would set up his own name, not as a repairer of the work but as the chief builder. Such folly are they guilty of who will set their own names before God's over the work of grace in their own souls. Oh, remember that boasting is excluded by the law of faith! Faith is that grace which empties the creature of all its conceited excellencies, and faith is that grace which will give God the praise of the glory of all His grace. Shall the groom of the stable boast of his master's horses, and the stage player of his borrowed robes? Shall the mud wall be proud that the sun shines upon it? We must say of all the good that is in us as the young man said to the prophet of his hatchet: "Alas, master, it was borrowed!" (2 Kings 6:5)

The church of God is compared to the moon. Now all the light which the moon gives to the world is only her distributing what is lent to her. All our graces, and the shining of them whereby our light is seen before men, are but a borrowed light from the Sun of righteousness. David sets an excellent pattern for us when he makes that humble acknowledgment in 1 Chronicles 29:10–14 and 16: "Blessed be Thou, Lord God of Israel, our Father for ever and ever. Thine, O Lord, is the greatness, and the power, and the glory, and the victory, and the majesty, for all that is in heaven or earth is Thine; Thine is the kingdom, O Lord, and Thou art exalted as head above all. Both riches and honor come of Thee, and Thou reignest over all; and in Thy hand is power and might, and in Thy hand is to make great and to give strength unto all. Now therefore, our God, we thank Thee and praise Thy glorious name. But who am I, and what is my people, that we should offer so willingly after this sort? For all things come of Thee, and of Thine own have we given Thee. O Lord our God, all this store that we have prepared to build Thee a house for Thine holy name cometh of Thine hand, and is all Thine own."

This is an excellent pattern of humility after enlargement in duty. David and the people had offered both bountifully and willingly towards the house of God. The Lord had enlarged both their hearts and their hands. Now all they did for God is here ascribed to God's grace and bounty towards them. It is excellent humility to ascribe our enlargement in God's service to the enlargement of God's grace towards us. The way to have grace increased is humbly to acknowledge from whence we receive every grace.

2. Ascribe unto Jesus Christ the glory of all the grace you have been made partakers of. Thus did Paul upon all occasions: "I labored more abundantly than they all, yet not I, but the grace of God which was in me, and by the grace of God I am what I am" (1 Corinthians 15:10). "I live, yet not I, but Christ

liveth in me, and the life which I now live in the flesh, I live by the faith of the Son of God" (Galatians 2:20).

It was well done of that good and faithful servant to say, "Lord, thy pound hath gained ten pounds" (Luke 19:16). He did not say, "Lord, my pains have gained this," but, "Thy pound hath gained."

When we give God the glory of His grace, God will give us the comfort and increase of our grace. Learn, therefore, to ascribe unto Christ the initial, progressive, and consummative work of grace in our souls. Jesus Christ only, who has begun a good work in you, will perform it until His own day. Jesus Christ is the author and finisher of our faith. He is the Alpha and Omega. And therefore the Apostle prays, "The God of all grace, who hath called us into His eternal glory by Jesus Christ, after that you have suffered a while, make you perfect, establish, strengthen, and settle you" (1 Peter 5:10).

Grace is rather like manna that comes from heaven than the corn which grows out of the earth. Grace is inspired from heaven. Gifts and parts are acquired by industry and pains here on earth. What God said by way of comparison between Canaan and Egypt is very applicable to this purpose. For thus God speaks to Israel: "The land whither thou goest in to possess it is not as the land of Egypt, whence thou camest out, where thou sowedst thy seed, and wateredst it with thy foot, as a garden of herbs, but the land whither ye go to possess it is a land of hills and valleys, and drinketh the water of the rain of heaven, a land which the Lord thy God careth for" (Deuteronomy 11:10–12). Thus it is with grace and nature. Nature may be, and is, improved with industry and pains, and is like Egypt, which might be watered by the foot, with digging gutters and trenches, which is the labor of the foot, to let in the streams of the river Nile when she yearly overflows her banks. But grace is like rain from heaven, which only falls when God appoints it: "Who causes it to rain upon one city and not upon another, and one piece is rained upon, and the piece whereupon it raineth not withereth" (Amos 4:7).

3. Disclaim all merit and self-sufficiency, for so much as we arrogate to our own merit, so much we derogate from the free grace and mercy of God. If, with Ephraim, God has enlarged His grace towards you that you are like a fig tree, yet let God have the glory of all your fruitfulness, and let Him say, "From Me is thy fruit found." Oh, consider that you do not bear the root, but the root bears you. Say, "Not unto us, O Lord, not unto us, but unto Thy name do we give the praise." A gracious heart knows his own inability, and his own insufficiency and imperfection, that he is unable to overcome the least sin though never so small; to exercise any grace though never so weak; to perform the least duty though never so easy. And as we have cause to acknowledge our inability, so also our sinful imperfections. If God should enter into judgment with us, He might condemn us not only for our worst sins but for our best duties.

4. Have an eye to Jesus Christ. Look up to Him, the author and finisher of our faith. The word "looking unto" signifies in the original such a looking as that we look away from those things which may divert our looking up to Jesus. Labor, my beloved, to look still unto Christ as the author of grace when you have the greatest exercise, or increase, or comfort of your grace.

Say when you have the greatest strength of grace, as
Jehoshaphat did when he had that great strength of
five hundred thousand men, "Lord, we know not what
to do, only our eyes are upon Thee" (2 Chronicles
20:12).

There are three things which we should eye in
Christ's giving us grace:

(1) How voluntarily and freely Jesus Christ issues out His grace to His people. Never did a mother
more willingly give her child suck, when her breasts
ached and were ready to break, than Jesus Christ bestows grace upon His people. Christ does not sell His
grace like a merchant, but, like a king, freely bestows
all.

See the tenor of the covenant, how free it was.
Isaiah 55:1: "Ho, every one that thirsteth, come ye to
the waters, and he that hath no money, come ye, buy
and eat; yea, come, buy wine and milk without money
and without price." Revelation 22:17: "Let him that is
athirst come, and whosoever will, let him take the
water of life freely." Nothing is so free as grace. It is
offered and bestowed upon the freest terms imagin-
able. All that Christ requires is but our receiving it. It is
the delight of Christ to show mercy and bestow grace
upon His people. It is the meat of Christ to do the will
of God who sent Him, and to finish His work. Never
was man more willing to eat his meat when he is hungry than Jesus Christ was to do good and bestow grace
upon him who lacked it. So also it is said of Christ in
Psalm 72:6 (which is clearly a prophecy of Jesus Christ)
that "He should come down like rain upon the mown
grass, and as showers that water the earth." Now there
is nothing that comes down more sweetly and freely

than rain upon a dry and thirsty ground.

(2) Secondly, look unto Jesus, the author of grace, how irresistibly He communicates His grace. "I will work, and who can let it?" (Isaiah 43:13). It is true not only of God's external deliverances, but it is as true of God's working grace in the hearts of His people. "Who shall let?"

Satan shall not, for though he is a strong man, and armed, and has possession, yet when Christ comes, He is stronger than Satan.

Sin shall not be able to hinder God's work of grace. Grace shall be too hard for the strongest opposition that is made against it. It is true that a man may, and does, resist the grace of God with a gainsaying and contradicting resistance, but not with an overcoming resistance.

(3) Third, look up to Jesus, the bestower of grace, how proportionately He gives grace suitable and answerable to your temptations and need. God divides to everyone His grace and gifts as He wills. And yet He gives grace that is enough. "My grace is sufficient for thee," God said to Paul; sufficient to quell corruptions, sufficient to repel temptation, sufficient to make you wait upon Me till I give you deliverance.

5. Be exhorted to have recourse to Jesus Christ for supply of grace. Go to Jesus and, by the prayer of faith, approach the throne of grace and beg grace to help you in time of need. Go to God by Christ, and God through Christ will supply all your wants. "My God," said Paul to the Philippians, "shall supply all your need according to His riches in glory by Jesus Christ" (Philippians 4:19). Go to this God and express yourselves before His throne with sensible complaints and

earnest requests. Say, "Lord, seeing there is so much water in the fountain, why should my cistern be empty? Such fullness of grace in Christ and so little grace in my heart? Lord, hast not Thou gifts for men, yea, for the rebellious also, and that is the worst that can be said of me, and hast Thou not a blessing for me also?"

USE OF CAUTION.

1. This should not cut off our endeavors after grace. We should so earnestly labor to get grace, as if there were no way to have it but by our endeavors. We should so strive to get heaven, as if it were to be gotten by our fingers, by our own pains. God's promises and purposes of giving grace should rather quicken and increase than in any way slacken our endeavors after grace. See how the Apostle makes God's working grace in us a ground why we should work: "Work out your own salvation with fear and trembling, for it is God which worketh in you both to will and to do of His good pleasure" (Philippians 2:12–13). And again, "I know the thoughts that I think towards you," said the Lord, "thoughts of peace and not of evil, to give you an expected end" (Jeremiah 29:11). But see how God joins their duty with His promise, the means unto the end: "Then shall ye call upon Me, and ye shall go and pray unto Me, and I will hearken unto you" (verse 12).

So also, in the prophecy of Ezekiel, the Lord had promised to do great things for them, and then adds, "Thus saith the Lord God, 'I will yet for this be inquired of by the house of Israel to do it for them' " (Ezekiel 36:37). God's promise to David to build him a house did not at all slacken his prayer to God for that purpose, for thus we find David praying, "Thou, O my

God, hast told Thy servant that Thou wilt build him a house; therefore Thy servant hath found in his heart to pray before Thee. And now, Lord, Thou art God, and hast promised this goodness to Thy servant; now, therefore, let it please Thee to bless the house of Thy servant, that it may be before Thee forever; for Thou blessest, O Lord, and it shall be blessed forever" (2 Samuel 7:27–29).

Thus also Paul said, "By the grace of God I am what I am, and His grace which was bestowed upon me was not in vain, but I labored more abundantly than they all, yet not I, but the grace of God which was in me" (1 Corinthians 15:10). See how he joins God's grace and his own endeavors together. You must then so endeavor after grace, as if it were to be gotten by labor and not bestowed by favor. Yet, when you have done all you can, you must acknowledge grace to be free, as if you had not labored at all.

2. Though there is an abundance of grace in Christ, yet let all such as have no interest in Christ take heed how they flatter themselves into a conceit that they shall receive grace from Christ. Interest in the person gives communication of His grace. As it was in Christ's person, He could not have had those excellencies and attributes which were in God, had not His two natures, human and divine, been personally united in Him. And therefore it is said, by virtue of the hypostatic union, that "in Him (i.e., in His person) dwelleth all the fullness of the Godhead bodily" (Colossians 2:9).

So unless there is that mystical union between Christ and us, we could not be partakers nor could we grow strong in the grace that is in Christ Jesus. Union is the ground of communion, and therefore we read first of "receiving Christ," and then afterwards of "receiving of His fullness grace for grace" (John 1:12, 16). Though you are near Christ by profession, yet, if you are not one with Christ by faith, you cannot receive any virtue from Him. If a man ties food to any part of his body, it will not nourish him because it is not received, digested, or incorporated. That only nourishes which becomes one and the same substance with us. So we receive strength and increase of grace from Christ as we are united to Him by faith.

Take a graft and tie it to a tree and it brings forth no fruit; but let it be united to a tree by implantation and then the graft grows fruitful. So, "without Christ (or, as it is in the original, separate from Christ) you can do nothing" (John 15:5). He who is not planted by faith in the likeness of Christ's death shall never receive spiritual nourishment from Him. He who does not abide in Christ is cast forth as a branch; he never was a true branch, he only seemed to be one.

Christ is a fountain of grace, but it is faith that draws out of this fountain. Christ is a treasury of grace, but it is faith that unlocks this treasury. By our communion with Christ we receive grace for grace. We are made by love meek and patient like Christ, but by faith we are made one with Christ. That union is the cause of communion, and therefore Christ-less persons are graceless persons.

3. If men lack grace, yet let them know that not Christ but they themselves are to be blamed. There is fullness in Christ. There is grace enough in Christ. In Him there is fullness of sufficiency, of efficiency, and of redundancy; but if a vessel is stopped, cast it into the sea and it will receive no water. Now the fault is in the

vessel which is stopped. There is no lack of water in the sea. Those who have their river water or conduit water coming into their houses, if no water comes, must not conclude there is no water in the river or the fountain, but that the pipes are either stopped or broken. So it is, if ever you are troubled, you are troubled in your own bowels, and not troubled in God. If a house is dark, it is not for any lack of light in the sun, but for lack of windows in the house. So if you lack grace, it is not for lack of grace in Christ but for lack of faith in your soul to draw and derive more grace from Christ.

4. Do not envy the grace of God in others. Though Christ should bestow more grace on others than you, "yet thy eye must not be evil because his is good." You should not have an envious eye because Christ has a bountiful hand. It is not only a fault in wicked men to envy the grace that is in good men (as Cain envied Abel because his sacrifice was accepted and his own rejected), but also good men are too apt to envy one another.

Joseph's brethren envied their brother because he was beloved of his father. Peter, it is thought, envied John, the beloved disciple. But take heed of envy. It is dishonorable to God and often hinders us from receiving mercy and grace from God. To envy Christ's dispensing of His grace to whom and in what measure He pleases is unbecoming a Christian. To rejoice in others' happiness is to do as the angels of heaven; to envy others' good is like the devils in hell. Would a father take it well that his children fall out about the portions which their father has given them? God is absolutely free to give one or two or five talents as He pleases; and if another has more grace than you, yet be thankful for that grace you have, and envy no man.

5. Last, do not lessen that grace you have received. As there is no small sin, because any sin is an offense against the great God, so there is no little grace, because it comes from the great God. Unthankfulness hinders this oil from running. As a man must not be contented with the greatest measure of grace, so he must not be unthankful for the least measure of grace. Consider, it is Jesus Christ who has begun the work of grace. That there is some little good wrought in you is the work of Jesus Christ, and He who has begun a good work will also finish it. He who has given grace a being in your soul will also strengthen you with strength in your soul and perfect what concerns you. Do not yourself quench the flax that begins to smoke, nor break the reed that is bruised. But be thankful to Christ who has kindled this smoking flax, and wait upon Him who will so accomplish His work that He will send forth judgment unto victory.